On The Midnight Train: Moscow to Leningrad

On The Midnight Train: Moscow to Leningrad

• MEMOIR, ESSAYS, PSYCHOLOGY, POETRY, THEATER •
ABOUT PROFOUNDLY DEEP-ROOTED CONFLICT AND AN
EVEN MORE FUNDAMENTAL YEARNING FOR PEACE

First Print Edition

Skip Robinson Ph.D.

© 2016 Skip Robinson Ph.D.

ISBN: 1532897227
ISBN 13: 9781532897221

The cover photograph was taken in Leningrad/St. Petersburg. It is of a large bronze statue of Tzar Petr the Great on horseback, Petr perhaps the central developmental figure in Russian history. Three hundred years ago, because he realized the central importance of increasing active Russian participation in European affairs, he commanded that Russia's ancient capital, Moscow, be physically moved West, much closer to Europe, to the current site of St. Petersburg, which Tzar Petr founded and had built through his own force of will, moving both the central governmental struc-tures and Russian society to a place originally a swamp but soon the center of state affairs. In spite of tremendous roadblocks, he finally succeeded. (For 70 years in the 20th Century St. Petersburg was renamed Leningrad.)

He also had deep feelings for the people and spent time regularly down at the docks, working with the sailors on their ships, building, exhorting, and helping raise the sails together. There, he was just like one of the other working men.

About
On the Midnight Train:
Moscow to Leningrad

"Dr. Skip Robinson, an international expert with remarkable skills in peace-building, and his colleagues have left through their team-work a palpable legacy wherever they worked together. The book is a great contribution to the history of conflict resolution and peace-building...."

U.S. Ambassador John W. McDonald, ret. and Chairman and CEO, Institute for Multi-Track Diplomacy (IMTD). Arlington VA

"For anyone who truly cares about striving to develop sustainable peace systems, Dr. Robinson [begins with] two memoirs on how it was possible to do so in a team approach between 1990 and 1996 in Russia and in Cuba. He not only recounts what occurred but relays the 'whys and hows' most conflicts often can be humanistically resolved..."

Bill Lincoln, Senior Lecturer, U.S. Naval Postgraduate School; Adjunct Faculty, U.S. Federal Executive Institute

[Regarding his poetry, of which there are five poems in this book]: "[Robinson's] poems often take place in the present tense, and they seek to move us, by way of the immediacies of his life, toward a powerful sense of real presence. His poetry continually opens us to the world."

Jack Foley, Editor, Poetry USA

*From Paul Tillich: "The first requirement of love
is to listen."*

Introduction

F or the first chapter, a memoir, the setting is late Spring 1990, Moscow and then Leningrad. This is a time when both Russia and the U.S. were in the process of declaring that the Cold War between their two countries and their alliances seemed to be over.

Our ecological negotiation and teaching team from the U.S., led by Bill Lincoln, had been invited to come to Russia to plan together with a Soviet team at Russia's largest Public Planning Institute (in the then-Soviet Union). We were coming to co-develop an intensive seminar with them to teach cooperative, democratic, interest-based conflict resolution skills meant to be offered to a variety of Russian professionals. This was an initiative encouraged by President Mikhail Gorbachev's central government, a then-new opening to the democratic West. This was apparently a wish on the central government's part to teach Russian professional people skills based in cooperative, democratic, interest-based values, using these communal skills to solve conflicts more humanely, as was then being done in an increasing number of countries around the world.

Descending into Moscow: Now, with a heightened roar, the Aeroflot Soviet Airlines plane bringing us in from Copenhagen is touching down at Moscow's Sheremetyevo Airport, bouncing once, rolling fast along the runway, slowing down as our plane rolls into the spot outside a gate where we are to park and unload. As our plane comes to its final stop at the gate, I look out my window and see, to my shock, that a single-file phalanx of Soviet soldiers, sharply dressed, shiny black boots, has moved into a semi-circle around the front of our plane, their rifles up and pointed this way. I think of the tens of thousands of thermonuclear weapons Russia and the U.S. have targeted on each other's cities and towns, way more than enough to end civilization and human life on the planet. The two countries poised: seeking peace with each other, yet with huge missiles on both sides rigid and poised, still considering aggression and war, even then, even when we thought the Cold War was over.

And there we are, struggling forward in the full airplane aisle, dragging our heavy luggage, walking out of the plane and walking into their world.

I think of the ancient Greek medical adage: "First, do no harm."

———⊗⊗⊗———

Late Spring 1990, Moscow, standing in massive, interminable airport customs waiting lines: We have come here to co-create a weeklong cooperative ecological negotiation seminar (to be offered the next spring) with a Soviet civilian team of professionals in Leningrad who all specialize in a host of related disciplines. The seminar is apparently set to become the first Soviet teaching on cooperative, interest-based, democratic ecological negotiation. We are here to plan the seminar with professionals from Lengiprogor, of Leningrad, pre-eminent Public Planning

Institute then responsible for public policy and operations in 500 Russian cities.

Now, today, it is late fall 2016. It's raining. I'm sitting at home. I watch on an on-line news program a video of Russian warships this week sweeping through the English Channel – a warning in the serious ratcheting up again of Russian-American tensions. Now people are talking of a new, growing Cold War: Expansive Russia grabbing and annexing its former possession, Crimea, part of Ukraine, another sovereign country now, (an action which immediately set off global condemnation with sanctions – invasion of another sovereign country, the takeover a taboo in Europe in the 21st century), Russian planes buzzing American warships. Russia leaving an important nuclear treaty. NATO moving to take more old former Soviet bloc nations into the Western alliance, Russian leadership computer hackers grabbing Democratic files to hound one side (through Wikileaks) to tip the U.S. Presidential election (new revelations showing an even more systematic apparently politically destructive presence), both sides planning, as a symbol and warning, to move onto both sides of Russia's borders even more thermonuclear weapons.

Each side is furious, with some justification, that the other side wants only to dictate (diktat) to them.

Hot off the press from CNN:

"'I think the world has reached a dangerous point,' the last leader of the Soviet Union Mikhail Gorbachev warned, according to <u>Agence France Presse</u>. 'This needs to stop. We need to renew dialogue,' Gorbachev said, commenting on the U.S. decision to call off Syria talks…' [The key issues for both sides need to be] nuclear disarmament, the fight against terrorism, the prevention of an environmental disaster,' he listed. 'Compared to these challenges, all the rest slips into the background.'"

""The quality of relations between us is certainly at the lowest point since the Cold War,' said Russia's Ambassador to the U.S. Sergey Kislyak. 'The risk of miscalculations has increased,' especially with NATO forces 'being deployed next to our borders,' Kislyak said in remarks at the Johns Hopkins School of Advanced International Studies. The ambassador said that 'normal channels of communication are frozen' between the U.S. and Russia."

It seems a very important time to study together.

—∞∞∞—

I've spent more than 50 years studying the psychology of humanistic peace and conflict resolution: in practice, in teaching, in ongoing dialogue with extraordinary colleagues, and in writing about all of these both here and abroad, both then and now. I want to try on these pages to share with you decades of experiences and findings. We are on the edge of unprecedented challenges and dangers.

We need to be thinking – and thinking together - about how we can cooperatively and deeply resolve conflict in more humane ways. Those who do so are likely to remain more satisfied from a humane, cooperative, and skilled approach. This, in turn, may give us much more durable settlements – something we need so very much.

—∞∞∞—

So, I begin the book with two international memoirs, written about earlier potential change points in Russia and Cuba in their relationships with the U.S. At those times, 26 years ago for Russia and 21 years ago for Cuba, the Cold War with Russia was seeming then to be coming to an end. Here was fast-improving communication and a feeling of hope on all sides.

Also, primarily in these first two chapters, five poems add dimension to those times we were experiencing there, written on site in Moscow and Leningrad/St. Petersburg, Russia, and in Havana, Cuba, where we were helping define cooperative conflict resolution with Cuba's Diplomatic Corps, as the Cuban Foreign Ministry prepared for more international change.

—∞∞—

The book begins with a poem on the astonishing crisis between 9/11 and the world.

Then, the first two chapters each share a memoir of our experience in dialogue in Russia and Cuba. Then come chapters on deepening our thinking through how to understand and resolve conflict – what skills we may need - what we may learn as people, citizens, educators, writers, and professionals across disciplines, between cultures, and across oceans seeking to work on how to work things out.

Thoughts in these essay chapters point toward a more systematic humanistic resolution of the healing of conflict and suffering, both in the family or workplace and between nations. They compare critical differences between methods of traditional adversarial negotiations and newer skills-building and perspective-building approaches for contemporary collaborative interest-based democratic negotiations. In this newer mix, a number of leading scholars in conflict work and in psychology add understandings.

Overall, these pages and chapters aim at some deeper ways for people to resolve conflict over time, especially in the midst of the startling transformations that are taking place now in each country around us.

Note that because of the startling and profound changes unfolding before us, we may need to consider how to negotiate with increasing pathological emergencies in public - in the wild cultural transitions here and to come.

Clearly, who we become is linked to how we negotiate with each other, where we stand, and how we treat others of our species and out to those of the wider living world, beings with individual and group lives of their own, who just don't happen to speak in our languages.

This yearning for peace lives deep in all of us, large and small, around our core, waiting to be roused, waiting to be made sense of, expressed, and put to work, to add to the forces toward peacemaking going on right here and all around the world and right now.

Overall, this book works on the premise that, in fact, we can learn to reach out together toward "peace in the valley".

About the memoirs

Chapter 1: Memoir on Russia and the Russians

First of all, we need to think back. 25 years ago, U.S.-Soviet Union/Russian attitudes were in a remarkably different state of change. Our then-U.S.-President George H. W. Bush, the Soviet Union's President Mikhail Gorbachev, and other public officials and public media world-wide declared, particularly when communism's rule in the Soviet Union finally ended in summer 1991, that this indeed signaled the end of the Cold War. The Berlin Wall had been knocked down in November 1989. With the wall coming down and the East's locked gates opening, television around the world showed people rushing out of East Germany into the West. And with that, enduring contact immeasurably increased. Much surprise and satisfaction. Long lost friends. Video showed us people climbing up on top of the wall and, piece by piece, knocking it down, smiling, cheering. We thought such walls seemingly would stay down forever.

A new era between our nations seemed ready to explore. At that time, a professional conflict resolution team from the U.S., led by Bill Lincoln, was asked to come there to collaboratively develop with a Soviet counterpart team a new and democratic (interest-based) approach to ecological conflict resolution. It was to be taught there in Leningrad (now St. Petersburg again), Russia to (and later by) Russian professionals working in a wide variety of professional fields – from law to education, from government to medicine, from psychology to labor, to diplomacy. As we understood it, the Gorbachev administration had decided to try experimenting with opening their professionals to a more cooperative and communal means of working through conflict, and, in this case, at first specifically working with ecological conflict.

Starting in late Spring 1990, our curriculum development and teaching team began going to Russia and, in the interims, corresponding with them on planning by e-mail. Then, for the first time, in late Spring 1991, we taught the seminar that we had jointly developed. The joint results were so successful, the resulting week-long full-time intensive seminar succeeded so strongly that the curriculum has subsequently been adopted by 25 Russian universities, building into the first Russian civilian undergraduate and graduate study programs in conflict resolution. (Their new term for this academic subject is Konfliktology.)

Chapter 2: Memoir on Cuba and the Cubans

21 years ago, the U.S. government and that of the Republic of Cuba were still struggling in the Latin American side of the Cold War. Over a number of months, at a distance and in person, a team from the U.S., Bill Lincoln's Conflict Resolution, Research and Resource Institute, Inc., (CRI), Tacoma, co-developed with Cuban diplomatic counterparts a full-time week-long cooperative, democratic (interest-based) conflict resolution seminar for their diplomats, scholars, and diplomats-in-training.

This memoir tracks each necessary step in the development of that seminar. We worked with the staff of the Cuban Foreign Ministry's *Institute Senior de Relaciones Internacionales* (ISRI) to develop and carry out the seminar, cultural and educational exchange, and research project.

As the development process began to grow, CRI added the Institute for Multi-Track Diplomacy, Inc., Arlington (IMTD), as a co-sponsor and retired U.S. Ambassador John McDonald as a co-teacher.

At that time, in 1994, as we understand it, President Castro had indicated that he might be interested in having Cuba's diplomatic corps explore a more cooperative approach to international negotiation.

After initial CRI negotiations with the Republic of Cuba together in Washington, D.C., the Cuban Foreign Ministry in Havana asked our team to co-plan with an ISRI-Cuban team a week-long, full-day dialogue exchange, research project, and conflict resolution seminar focused on increasing skills in cooperative, interest-based, democratic conflict resolution approaches – a seminar among U. S. negotiation professionals and Cuban diplomats, scholars, and senior diplomats-in-training. The team from the U.S., from CRI, IMTD, and the ISRI Cuban team were to plan the seminar at-a-distance working together.

Then the team director from the U.S. would, when the time was right, come to Havana, in cooperation with the *Instituto Superior de Relaciones Internacionales (ISRI), Havana,* do final planning and readiness work with ISRI, and then the full teams would come together to carry out the seminar – *cooperative, interest-based, democratic research project, on conflict resolution: our team of conflict resolution professionals meeting for a week with Cuban diplomats, international Cuban government officials,, and each other. (As it worked out, according to Likert scale questionnaires which we asked each participant to fill out periodically through each seminar day, the first day went fine, and each day proved better than the one before, ending in scores on Friday for the week as a whole of 96% participant positive evaluation of the seminar's pertinence and satisfactions.) Everyone involved felt the dialogue brought more trust, shared clarity, more skills to communicate with. Hard to leave Havana; good to be coming home.*

These memoir pages seek to take the reader through our own living and thinking as those planning and teaching days developed and came to pass, the thoughts, emotions, surprises which kept emerging among us from the work together.

It turns out, as shown in the first two chapters filled with the chronicles of memoir, those developments over two decades ago can point light toward the character, hopes, and strategies in our lives today. The later chapters offer perspective and skills to carry forward. And in light of the utterly wild uproar in which we now find ourselves living, we can choose to search for more ways for ourselves, our families, our working groups, for an opening heart, and for new perspective, with us determined to find and develop personally and diplomatically open environments which can aim, for today and for our children's children, toward a more peaceful, sustainable future home and world.

If we choose, we can certainly grow and head in that way.

———∞∞∞———

One Cuban participant, on the seminar's last afternoon, said:

"Wouldn't it be wonderful if conflict resolution became another language of the world. If everyone had the same language, and before they resorted to force and violence and treachery to resolve disputes – would say, wait, there's another way to do this. Let's sit down. Let's see if we can negotiate this and have your interests and my interests somehow be satisfied."

———∞∞∞———

Table of Contents

Part 2: Thinking about conflict

*The poem by Skip Robinson below is reprinted with permission from the award-winning collection of a number of poets, Josephine Miles PEN Prize for poetry, **An Eye for an Eye Makes the Whole World Blind – Poets on 9/11**, Regent Press, Oakland, edit by Allen Cohen and Clive Matson*

Back the night before

yearn for the huge silver airliners to pull backwards out of the buildings they've slammed into, for the knives to retreat from the flesh as if they had never thought of entering, that the blades return to their box-cutting, with no move to the left or the right.

I plead with the explosions to return back into their bombs, their hand grenades, their mortar shells, taken back apart again, back into the airplanes filled with fuel for the long journey home. I plead that the great expanses of rubble and broken stone rise back up into the buildings they had been before the attacks, the roads back into being, leading again to the homes of loved ones. I beseech the blood, the pieces of flesh, the eyes, the guts, the skin, the organs of love-making to float up from deep in the rubble soil and weave themselves back into the living bodies of family and community. I cry that we gain the determination to climb back before all the deathly events, back the night before, the night of September 10th, while the angry and oppressed are talking outside, inside other people are talking and listening with each other over dinner - how to live fairly with each other, how to live fairly with the planet, how to bring those outside in - the next day the same people climbing onto the same airliners, flying successfully through to their destinations, the balance of things swinging back toward a fair center, minds flooding with visions of a new century and millennium beginning. I reach my hands up toward the sky and plead that cooling rain fall down, that a bright moon may rise into the black sky, that all the stars are luminous against the backdrop of utter darkness, that the families are all safe and home again, and that the only fires are in their fireplaces and in the stars.

CHAPTER 1

On the Midnight Train: Moscow to Leningrad

t is late on a spring night, very chilly in the hour just before midnight, May 1990, Moscow's central railroad station, getting colder as full night settles in. Fresh air flowing through the huge dome. Dark outside, yet, somehow, the sky still glows with muted light.

Around the world is California and the U.S. Around me in this huge echoing train station, I hear language sounds I'm not used to, only Russian and Slavic tongues I think, plus the language of huge loud machines – and pungent smells from trains periodically fill the place. Big puffs of white smoke. Very loud squeaks and squeals from the behemoth trains pulling in. The group of us from the U.S., our ecological negotiation studies team, utterly exhausted, has just spent fourteen hours in the air, mainly over the Atlantic Ocean – On Alitalia from San Francisco through New York and straight on to Copenhagen, then on Aeroflot (the Soviet airline) from Copenhagen to Moscow. (The Aeroflot attendants threw us sandwiches almost as you would throw a baseball.) This last flight was about three hours. We landed in Moscow in late afternoon. Tonight at midnight we would take the famous midnight train to Leningrad, where we would be working/studying, preparing a full-day ecological and public policy negotiation simulation jointly with Soviet Russian colleagues. (That ecological negotiation simulation play (to be developed into an improvisation drama) would be played out for the first time a year from then, on the last day of the week-long seminar.)

As our Aeroflot flight was taxiing up to the gate in Moscow, I found, looking out my oval window, a large contingent of Soviet soldiers on the tarmac directly in front of us, in khaki with high shiny boots, holding rifles at the ready. That very day, I thought, thousands of thermonuclear missiles were still aimed at the cities and towns of each other's country - Thousands of potential Hiroshimas. The Berlin wall has just recently fallen. Gorbachev was instituting major new national policies, Glasnost and Perestroika, aimed at truth-telling by the government (which had been tested after Chernobyl) and thorough restructuring of their economy and their political methods.

After enduring interminable airport security and swimming through utterly huge, pushy crowds, we finished entering the country and finally pushed out the airport's front doors into fresh early night air. Just outside the airport we joined six Moscow-Leningrad colleagues and counterparts. Early evening – taken to a handsome restaurant - our choices of several kinds of borscht, salads, meats, good bread, excellent dinner in the midst of our new joint experiences - English and Russian being spoken tentatively together, some acting as interpreters. Our cordial professional colleagues are staying with us here in Moscow until we are ready to go meet our train. They will wait until the huge shiny black Midnight Train to Leningrad steams in, until we climb aboard, until we head off into the deep midnight headed toward Leningrad, due to arrive there just about dawn.

We're so very tired and sleepy. The storied Midnight Train from Moscow to Leningrad is due to arrive soon to take us there, but in our exhaustion we feel that it's been such a long time we've been standing waiting on the railroad platform they've taken us to. The train is due and we are waiting half-asleep, deep in jet lag, in fact, more asleep than half. I would so gladly fall into bed in a hotel right now; but we are to go to our destination tonight; and we really must go. We will meet our counterparts soon after dawn.

Our own U.S. group 's particular focus is on co-creating with our Russian counterparts, a full-day ecological negotiation simulation (essentially an improvisational drama) to be played out by Soviet seminar participants late spring of the following year on the last full day of the seminar we will be planning: Soviet regional planners, scientists, psychologists, negotiators, architects, engineers, public representatives, city and "oblast" (county) executives, lawyers, and others. It was to be a multi-disciplinary, active, and dramatic visceral synthesis of the week's collaborative conflict resolution learning process.

We were to be working with Leningrad's Lengiprogor, at that time the Soviet Union's largest Russian public planning institute at that time had full city planning responsibilities for over 500 Russian cities.

I'm utterly drained, exhausted, near midnight, flight-addled, still, still standing next to my bags. I look down at the railroad platform. Well-washed black and gray marble floor. I want so much to sit down and go to sleep right now. The nearby locomotive diesel engines give off a loud bass hiss and a strong oily electrical smell.

The odors and heat come in waves. The intensity of the railroad sounds and smells around us increases ten-fold as the Midnight Train appears some distance away and begins pulling in on the track toward us.

The Moscow-to-Leningrad midnight train is huge, pulls up on the track right in front of us. With a great loud shudder, the train stops, issuing forth loud bangs of the metal railroad car couplers, very loud metal-on-metal steely squeaks, then a long very loud pneumatic hiss. Then relative quiet.

A trainman rolls the metal climb-up stairs into place below our train entrance door, connecting us on the platform with the high entrance to the shining railroad car now right in front of the group of us. From the side of this passenger car, bright yellow Cyrillic letters reach out to us in print. I stare and wonder intensely what I they mean.

Uniformed trainmen walk up, bow, and tell us in Russian to please climb up the metal stairs to our railroad car's high entrance. They point up the stairs. They are encouraging, well dressed. The railroad car's steel steps are steep, and our feet make metal clacking noises as we climb up. This railroad car appears well washed and in good and rather shiny condition tonight. It is finally midnight. (So long – two days - since the last real sleep at home.) At the top of the steps, I take in the intense smell of hot metal and oil and walk inside.

Down the car's narrow wooden and steel corridor, Jon Townsend and I (Jon, from Portland, Oregon, is my fellow teacher and curriculum developer on this journey and in the future) carry our heavy bags, made so much heavier by our walking the hallway in a half-dozing state. Beyond the approaching door to our space, at the far end of the car's hallway, we can see a large silver Russian samovar, a beautiful old-fashioned water boiler, polished and shining against the far wall, ancient tradition, ready with its ornate spigot to pour steaming hot water for one's coffee or tea. An old white-coated attendant stands by the samovar. He regards us with a nod and a bow.

Toward the end of the hallway is a small cabin on the right to which we have been assigned. I open the door and put the bags inside. Wooden slat benches stick out from the opposite sides of the room, a bench place on opposite sides, one for each of us. I see a rack above me and reach up and stow my belongings, hopefully for the night. Tomorrow seems so far away, almost a dream.

The hard slat benches stuck out just about twelve to fourteen inches from the opposite walls. Apparently the only place to sleep. No cushion or mattress in sight. No sheets. No pillow. No blankets. So I'll use sweaters., coat, rolled up clothes for a pillow, another coat laid down for a cover. Cold still, holding tight with one hand to the outside slat to keep me from falling off the bench onto the floor in the railroad car sway of my sleep. Floods of thoughts. Please let the sleep come soon.

Lying still, I found myself wondering more about this profoundly different culture we were about to try to learn with, a country wrapped with us in vast and deadly paradoxes. (Now we were beyond the books, correspondence, lengthy planning. Here we were on Russian soil. But the sides still poised entwined near the edge of abyss:

Dan Ellsberg at the Lama Foundation, Summer weekend conference, 1984

"...but between '55 and '60, we retooled. We modernized. We put in Teller's bombs, H-Bombs, same [U.S. nu-
clear] plans to hit the same cities – and the (projected)
casualties ([n a full nuclear war] went from 20 million to
600 million, first strike; and, sort of, nobody noticed."

I continued to lie there. The rumbling of the train's wheels on the
track became soothing. But sleeping was coming so very hard. For
a long time I lay there tossing, turning, tossing some more. Sleep
seemed to become agonizingly impossible. Then hours fitfully in
and out of exhausted semi-consciousness, sleeping, the wheels of
the train ever clicking and waving below us. The hard thin bench
beneath me was moving and moving with the hard constant motion of the train on the tracks. Even relatively unconscious, I was
still trying to hold on, to be sure I didn't fall off the bench. Then
half dreams – the thermonuclear war threat and nowhere to hide.
Then another dream feeling that somewhat distant possibility that
this trip could work, could help with more resolution of conflict,
explorations in developing more joint conflict resolution language and concepts. Failing into deeper sleep exploring what it
might feel like for us, ending our wars, what it might feel like for
us all during the first night that everyone on earth has been fed,
knowing that there was already enough for all. (Tonight, says the
World Bank, over 900 million are hungry.) Vaguely, falling into
sleep, so groggily worrying, trying at least not to make things any
worse between us all.

When, early in his being Premier, then-Soviet President
Gorbachev brought out a national policy he called
"Glasnost," or truthful public reporting, one critical truth
which soon began to spread around the world was the very
extent of Soviet and Eastern European environmental
poisoning.

Mr. Gorbachev's parallel initiative, "Perestroika," involved planning to functionally restructure the Soviet social order, so that it was more humane, effective, safe, looking for more justice for the Soviet people. Basic to their future in successful dealing with their environmental crisis would be the negotiation of plans for the resolution of ecological crises, the development and preservation of ecological balance, and the revitalization of that which had already been severely ecologically damaged and which was presently in great danger of becoming much worse. The Russians wanted to train more people in ecological negotiation, to develop an ecological negotiation momentum and tradition.

They were also dealing with new and fascinating democratic issues in general and also with who to consider as logical parties to sit at any ecological negotiation table, under what circumstances, with what objectives. They needed to refine and keep focused on the utter gravity of their Russian ecological predicament, developing strategies to move them beyond those mortal dangers.

—⊂∞∞⊃—

I woke up to faint light against my eyelids, gentle light coming in the cabin's small window. With some effort and grunting, I finally sat myself up. I began working on getting that special balance again of standing up on a bouncing, fast-moving train, gently shaking back and forth, sounding and bouncing to the clack-clack on the rails. I stood up and, blinking, began to look around. More light. I walked over, balancing carefully, and opened the cabin door to the hallway. With the door open, I heard the deep sounds of the train and the tracks increasing ten-fold. I looked out along the long naturally lighted hallway, gleaming samovar inviting at our end of the car. I walked along the hallway toward the railway car's center. Several travelers, including a couple of our colleagues, had gathered there, standing with others silently staring out the big car's panoramic hallway windows. There lush Russian countryside rolled by in the foggy early light. Nobody talking. Only the sound and feel of the big steel wheels rolling on the track beneath us. The sight of endless lovely green forest life rolling by outside, mile after mile.   Waking up some more. The sun's coming up some more. All so massive, so beautiful. Gray forest fog growing less intense in the emerging light. This would be the day. Today we arrive.

As the train approached the increasingly urban area, before the train quite reached Leningrad and the railroad station, all of us got up and moved around, groggy, getting fully dressed, re-packing all our belongings to be ready to go. Then out to the hallway, the green, brown, and the lightening blue outside, almost a blur, the moaning sound of our train. Everyone fell quiet - and watched Leningrad Station began to arrive ahead and then pull around us.

As we pulled forward - loudly squeaking brakes – into the station, ornate, bright. Looking out the hallway windows, we first saw drawing toward us, as the train slowed down, a group of maybe twenty standing on the platform. We guessed right that it was our hosts from the Lengiprogor City/State Planning Institute. They were standing there as a group on the approaching platform area, smiling, spouses and children standing beside them, beginning to wave.

The train stopped, loud clattering and steam venting. We climbed off, and we met. Here was my host, a tall thin Lengiprogor architect, Alexandr Chiburyn, his wife, Nina, an engineer, and their teenage daughter, Masha, a high school student. (At that time, I had two teenage daughters of my own at home.) I was to stay with the Chiburyns during our work together.

So we walked together out of the station, walked for some distance, and climbed onto public transit to cross the city to their apartment. The Leningrad public transit we took was impressive - fast, frequent we understood, clean, positive. We reached their apartment, met their family dog, Jack, a big German shepherd who knew he was their big protector, and settled in, had good hot tea from their kitchen's steaming samovar and then had a home-cooked dinner of beef and potatoes. Masha, their daughter, pulled out their Russian-English dictionary (called in Russian a Slovar); I pulled out one I'd gotten at home, among the materials I had been studying toward this day. We began to talk, a word or phrase at a time. Wife and daughter knew no English, but Masha was good with a Slovar, and Alexandr knew some English and they made it all work.

When Alexandr turned on their television set, in Russian and English, we heard "Who You Gonna Call?" On the screen appeared a Russian language version: <u>Ghostbusters</u>.

⸎

So there we were, Masha, Alexandr, Nina, Jack, and me. My body had come to a complete stop in a soft chair in their kitchen. I felt good about being with them, sitting around the table, family life centered there in the kitchen, the samovar bubbling sounds across the room, Jack curled up knowingly on the kitchen floor.

Leningrad in Russian is pronounced approximately Leen-in-gradya. To me, at this beginning, I experienced Leningrad as a warm kitchen, with a kind family, people I would stay with for the couple of weeks of work. And Alexandr and I would be working together.

Over dinner, we got into a lively cross-language exchange, looking to our two-language dictionaries for apt words or phrases with which to query or answer each other. Especially Masha. We stayed at it for an hour. Then I began to fold.

Alexandr took me to their living room, where he put together their pull-out bed into the living room space, a rather comfortable bed, I was happy to learn – finally the promise of a full night of sleep in a real bed. After flying out from San Francisco two days ago, in just a few minutes, I was finally under very warm covers. I thought about the home and the country I had left to come here. Things began to blur, to fade away, then long deep sleep.

Alexandr woke me up at 7. It was to be our first work day together.

Time for me to shower and get dressed and ready to go. "Oh", Alexandr said: "Be sure to shower with your mouth closed. Don't let any shower water get in. You really mustn't swallow any. And don't use spigot water for brushing teeth." My mind spun with what that must mean.

I hardly remember breakfast. There we were - out the door – the first day bright as we began walking briskly toward the tram.

Alexandr and I walk at a good pace for ten minutes or so to the tram stop. It's a bit cloudy, I remember. We talk a bit as we walk, with Alexandr offering his English. It's hard but he perseveres. Good man.

The tram pulls up in front of us soon and stops. Their trams are rather thin, much like ours at home and in Europe. It is almost full. We stand and hold onto ceiling straps as the tram moves forward, headed for the nearest subway station, gets there, and stops. Everyone gets off and walks toward the subway station entrance. The subway station is big and clean, distinctive art patterns reach out from the wall tiles as we enter. The individual subway fare is equivalent to a U.S. penny. We head to the escalator in a mass and begin going down to the platform far below. It's a long ride down. The platform walls continue the station's ceramic and tile. Quite lovely. The freshly washed subway train arrived within five minutes and stopped in front of us. We got on and took hold of ceiling straps again; the car was full. In Russian, an amplified voice was asking that people move completely inside the car, that the door was about to close. Then, on that first day, I didn't understand a thing. But I started a pattern of inquiry. "Alexandr, what was that announcement? What does this word mean? What's the Russian word for that? (I started to listen and learn those words in Russian. We'd be at this for two weeks. I ought to learn.) Alexandr was very patient explaining things to me. The ceiling of the subway car was graced, above us, along its ceiling spine. A half dozen big beautiful lights, with pink concentric circles around the glass. So like surreal oversized nipples. Most people took no notice that Alexandr and I were speaking a very basic English. The talking all around us sounded Russian or Slavic. The announcement came on that we were about to arrive at our station. Alexandr led the two of us through the doors, into the mass moving toward the escalators, up for a long ride, then through the busy station and out the door. We began walking toward the Lengiprogor Planning Institute, the offices we would be meeting in almost every day for two weeks.

We were to be working on planning and writing together with their team toward developing an all-day improvisational ecological and public planning negotiation simulation. This simulation was to be played out by Soviet participants for the final day of the week-long full-time seminar to be offered the next spring or summer.

The walking to work was helping me wake up (though jet lag was to come and go for days). As we walked up to the Lengiprogor front entrance, Alexandr opened the door for me and was smiling. In English: "Here's home," he said.

When Gorbachev was head of the Soviet government, terms glasnost and perestroika were ubiquitous reporting in American papers. The Chernobyl nuclear plant mega-disaster seemed to begin to show a significant change around Soviet public policy, dropping propaganda in favor of accurate reporting around Chernobyl. For example, after about a week of the usual obfuscation, in a seeming major break from old policy, the Soviet Government suddenly began releasing seemingly accurate radiation and damage data right away, data which was very valuable for other nations to use to independently assess the situation and what danger they might be in. The whole world was frightened about possible radiation spreading. The government's candor was shocking because the West was used to smoke and mirrors, and the West had gotten used to getting spin and propaganda from Soviet obfuscation.

Glasnost called for truth-telling among agencies of the Soviet government and between those agencies and the Soviet and world publics. Perestroika, in Russian literally restructuring. The policy called for major reorientations and restructuring of the national government, toward more transparency, more listening, more judicious and equitable, democratically directed problem resolution, more shared power and responsibility. It was in the frame of this opening change that we had been asked to come over. We were asked to collaboratively develop with them a week-long seminar on cooperative (non-dictatorial) ways of ecological conflict resolution. This seminar would be given for a wide variety of public leadership. Leningrad University would be brought into the potential for educational leadership there.

⸺⸺

The first session of our Lengiprogor U.S. team took place in a large room on the second floor at Lengiprogor where a number of small tables had been formed into the shape of a circle, accommodating about 40 of us. I looked around the room at the faces of the Lengiprogor team at the table. It strikes me that it could just about as easily be an ecological professionals' group meeting at home. Their team was about equally male and female, a variety of racial and ethnic backgrounds, both young and several stages of middle-aged.

Then we began. Greetings in both languages. We started around the room with each person on the Russian team talking briefly about their work and recent focus. Each one related professional focus on critical ecological dangers, often in what had been great personal risk. Ever since then, I've thought often about that meeting as one of heroes and heroines – soil scientists, biological scientists, architects, lawyers, psychologists, public policy analysts, city and regional administrators, educators, and others. What was pouring out was this combination of a wide variety of professional disciplines showing their own ways of moving the system they were working in toward more cooperative approaches, joint research, ones which honored honesty and reform. In the recent past, before Gorbachev, Glasnost and Perestroika, many had put their jobs (and possibly their freedom and their lives) on the line in order to report, study, and correct ecologically destructive practices. What was most common in these tales was principled dialogue and action. Our team had known through Western media about Gorbachev's declaring these radical new goals, about their first attempts to carry these new goals forward. Yet we had not seen the flow of critically important public change going on as a result - and at the same time, right at the society's grass roots. Now, here it was. And here we were.

Later that afternoon, the teams developing the eco-negotiation program (team problem-solving) first broke into work groups, with our group focusing on the full-day improvisational drama we would develop, which would be for all seminar participants most of the last full day of the week-long seminar, playing out the cooperative ecological negotiation simulation (or it could be called an improvisational drama) which would give them the opportunity to put together and use all that they had been learning that week about collaborative basic-human-needs ways of negotiating – an ecological negotiation simulation involving the development of cooperative public planning around an ecological crisis and multiple-party decision-making.

Cemetery

At one point, as the plans began to develop, we went out together to the Leningrad war memorial which had mass graves from World

War II, Adolf Hitler's troops attacked and, in a hideously long siege, surrounded Leningrad, continuously bombed it, left everyone there starving, squeezed it like a fiendish boa constrictor. Hitler's siege lasted 900 days, two and a half years. In my mind now, I still see mass grave mounds one after another after another, each mound about fifty feet wide by 100 feet long, about 2500 Leningraders to a mound, some mounds marked civilian, some military, some mounds marked 1941, some 1942, some 1943, rows upon rows upon rows. There, I counted up to 100,000 civilian mass graves in just one area (the counting took only a minute). Then I stopped, sat down, did not move for a long while, the sky cloudy, the vast silence of the dead.

"Hero-City" says a main metal memorial held in stone across the front of the last rows of mass mounds, "Mother Leningrad".

It is becoming cold. I stand there. Beyond the mass grave mounds, headed in one direction, the older historic three-hundred year old St. Petersburg graveyard goes back through the great foliage there and disappears out of sight.

Babushka on the bus

As soon as I could learn to make my way, with very rudimentary Russian and with basic directions, I began to go out on my own through the city on buses and trams. One day, in a bus crammed full of riders, I was standing, holding the strap overhead, next to an old woman, wearing a traditional babushka over her head, carrying a large bulky purse at her side. (These old women themselves are commonly called "babushkas". As the bus made its way along, at one moment she reached down into her big bag. Some riders nearby turned surreptitiously to look. Her hand pulled up, out of the bag, the happy face of a little black and white puppy, who immediately looked around with interest and woofed. Laughter broke out around her. The laughter quickly spread through the bus. People craned their necks to see. The babushka was obviously, shyly pleased. Nearby, a young couple, he in military uniform, she in pretty checkered dress, laughed and, still chuckling, kissed each other. The babushka and her dog were not our enemy. Nor were those others, laughing, smiling, pointing. I yearned that they be taken out of our thermonuclear bomb sights. This, these people, after all, as it was turning out in my feelings, were honestly part of our family.

Another bus ride

Another day, when I was riding on another bus, looking out at the every-dayness of those walking along outside, the buildings behind them. I had been studying the Russian written language and its Cyrillic alphabet for some time but had no uses for it yet. (That alphabet had been developed for the Russians from the Greek a thousand years ago.) My bus was stopped for traffic. I looked outside at a store's large Cyrillic sign. To me, gibberish, I thought. Then, on impulse, I took the word across letter by letter. The first Russian letter was like our P. The second like our R. The third Cyrillic letter in the sign was like our O. Suddenly, like a flash, I saw form the word PRODUCE. I looked and saw lettuce and cabbage stacked in the front window. Here was a word (called a cognate) where two languages have a word or phrase in common (after you get through the fog, through the Cyrillic alphabet). Suddenly, everything was less of a mystery. Things could, after all, be learned. There were matters in common. There was hope.

• Rybachye is born

'In the region of Primor'ye, on the eastern shores of the Confederation of Independent States, just off the Sea of Japan, is the seacoast town of Rybachye. Located between Vladivostok and Dal'negorsk, Rybachye has enjoyed a relative quiet and peaceful existence for many years." So began the description the Russian-American team was drafting for the ecological negotiation simulation drama we had come to develop. The title became "The Problems of Developing the town of Rybachye – Scenario of the game for teaching the method of negotiating on disputable problems of regional planning and nature protection". As we alternatively drafted and met in committee to consider the drafts, the background reading for all negotiation game participants (the negotiation seminar participants) grew to almost 30 pages, including reports of an eye-opening initial meeting of Rybachye resident•

In our small working group, we were tackling the question of what, in our ecological simulation (our improvisational drama) the crisis we were thinking through would be about. Who would be the set of characters in the drama? Who and what would they represent? How would they have to struggle in the search for common ground with their adversaries? Slowly in our discussions a pattern began to emerge. This would have to be a struggle of ideology and action among the different groups with a primary interest in a sustainable ecological solution which they could share. Perhaps an important mining discovery, but one which could have extremely negative ecological consequences. Something paradoxical.

White nights

In Russia, geographically high up North on the earth's globe, much nearer the North Pole, an effect is, in the winter, significantly fewer hours of light, and, in summer, significantly more hours of light. (In early summer, at 11 pm, cars run along Leningrad streets with no headlights on, the atmosphere of gauzy light remaining in the sky, giving rise to an annual early summer festival in Leningrad (now St. Petersburg again) called White Nights. My hosts, the Chibouryns, introduced me to it. After we had been working at Lengiprogor for a few days, they suggested that I take an early evening nap. They would get me up again at 11 pm. The whole family would be going to go across the city and down to the banks of the flowing Neva River, in front of the Winter Palace. The tradition was to arrive at the river by midnight. They woke me up at 11 pm. They were in a festive mood, joking, smiling, laughing, packing for a picnic. We left home and walked together in this 11 pm twilight with ever-increasing groups of others toward the tram stop. The mass of the group was building as we walked, every-one seeming to be in a holiday mood. We wedged onto the tram, headed off through the cool evening air, and soon arrived at the subway stop. We got off into the growing crowd converging on it. We entered for a kopek and headed down the long escalator. The platform below was filling with those waiting for the downtown/ Winter Palace train.

At the end of our subway journey, when we came out of the subway door and came up the long escalator, we walked with thou-sands of others just a few blocks together along a huge triumphal square and the Winter Palace and, as we turned a corner, began to see the wide Neva River all deep blue and rippling before us. We walked toward it, past the breathtaking white and light blue Winter Palace and came down to a spot on the bank of the river.

We chose a place to sit along the Neva's banks, and spread out our picnic cloth. More and more people, too, gathered, sat down, and spread picnics out on checkered cloths on the grass at the banks of the flowing river. At midnight, the bridges across the riv-er raised to let big ships come in to port from the Bay of Finland, just north. (Ships could come into the Neva during the first hour, midnight to 1 am, to unload. Ships could go back out during the second hour, from 1 to 2 am.

A brightly dressed wedding couple came walking through the midnight gathering, tossing flowers, smiling broadly, and responding happily to the enthusiastic applause and cheers of the crowd. Jugglers, actors, musicians came by our spot on the grass. The huge ships flowed by. On the shore, the star-lit night around us; the picnicking folks around us began to sing.

Rybachye takes form

The night before the negotiation simulation game we were developing was to be played (during the week of the seminar to be held the next spring/summer), the game participants were to read what we came to call the Common Data Bank. Each of the four teams we decided to have playing (1. Rybachye town citizens team, 2. Russian Republic's Ministry of Economics team, 3. The Ministry of Industry team, and 4. the local Fisheries/Tourism team, each would have its own priorities and interests. Our collaborative working team continued drafting, writing out outlines for team and individual player descriptions. The Rybache simulated negotiation game was taking shape.

Another ride on the tram

One day, riding the tram, thinking I had reached the stop for "home", I in fact got off a couple of stops too soon, but I didn't then realize it. I thought I knew my way back, but when I looked around carefully, I found the surroundings strange, unknown. I asked a young woman passing by if she spoke any English. "Just a tiny bit," she said. (I knew very, very little Russian, not enough to get out of this.) I thought to explain my plight, but I could see by her face that she understood only a little of what I was trying to say. I asked her if she knew any French (which I had studied a bit in high school and college). "Nyet," (no) she said in Russian. Then she said: "Just wait a minute." She went off and disappeared. I felt so very vulnerable and miserable standing there lost.

She came right back, smiling broadly. She had with her a neighbor who spoke a little French, as well as his native Russian. So we began to talk, haltingly, together – Russian to French to English and back and forth. They realized that I was lost after getting off the neighborhood tram at the wrong stop. They walked me back to the tram stop. We talked and gestured about where I was going. Soon, I was getting on the next tram, thanking them both vividly, sincerely, hoping I was now remembering the characteristics of the stop I was rushing toward. Thankfully, I did recognized the right stop when we got there. I got off. A little walk I remembered and soon I was safe at "home". At the front door, Jack greeted me with a friendly knowing woof.

⚭

Early one morning as I was just coming out of dreams, a story line for the negotiation simulation began to emerge in my mind: On a bright cold Saturday morning, a quite young Russian girl was to be out enjoying and exploring a lush woods in a Forest Preserve with her engineer father.

She is now walking alone, following a path of flowers among sunlight shafts floating down from between the tree branches high above, when she notices a bright outcropping, apparently a vein of something metal, perhaps uncovered by the recent much-harder-than-usual rains. The vein is so pretty that she calls to her father. He ambles over, smiles at her, and looks down.

The story line begins to unfold. Strategic metal (in national short supply), particularly delicate ecosystem above the city's aquifer. Mining for the nationally important metal could endanger the city and region's water supply and cause dangerous pollution. But the metal is needed. Traditional rules apply. New rules apply. What applies? Our working team began discussing this and other plot line proposals. Ideas flowed into the brainstorming session that followed. Things were beginning to take further shape.

Requiem

One night, our Russian hosts took us to a very special event, at the Smolny Institute (the first state-financed higher education institution for women in Europe, built by Katherine the Great).

This was to be the first singing in Russia, since the 1917 Revolution, of Rachmaninoff's "Requiem" by the great Leningrad chorus., (A requiem, according to Webster's, is a mass for the repose of the souls of the dead, in this case a national act of remembrance.)

Rachmaninoff's "Requiem" had been banned by the Soviets ever since it was written, as part of the harsh and often brutal repression of dissent, many decades ago.

Now here we are. Perestroika and Glasnost in effect, the world-class Leningrad Chorus in blue robes singing with the power of real, deep, profoundly resonating words in celestial music.

Sadness in immense personal and national loss. Joy in determination to go on.

The Russians were so anxious for us to begin to understand their love of art. This performance was doing just that. We walked out afterwards into snow falling. Feeling for the dead. Thinking of the living. Sensing the open future.

Such significant Russian art was all around us. Every time I came to Leningrad creating the drama and then being a team member teaching the resulting seminar, I began going to the Hermitage. We knew that Katherine the Great, who reined in the late eighteenth century, had created a unique and world-class art museum called the Hermitage in her beautiful Winter Palace. (She had sent her representatives all around European capitals seeking the best paintings and sculpture. They were extraordinarily successful. Imagine whole rooms filled with Rembrandts, Fauvist paintings exploding off the museum walls upstairs, some of the world's best art. I began going there, climbing the massive, curving white marble stairs.

Premier writiers such as Dostoevsky, Tolstoy, Chekov created an extraordinary set of stories and books at the end of the 19th Century for us to read and be stunned.

Nevsky Prospekt

Soon after we arrived, our hosts took us for a long walk along one of their great boulevards, perhaps the city's best. Nevsky Prospekt. Prospekt in Russian means a major thoroughfare with wide vistas. Alexandr Nevsky was one of Russia's greatest early warriors and one of its most important historical figures, named in his heroism for the Neva River which flows through town. Nevsky means "of the Neva". Hundreds of years ago, he led his warriors against tremendous odds to save Russia at the last moment in the last great battle.

We walked along Nevsky Prospekt together observing the people walking along there, too. In so many ways, we seemed so similar, yet so distinct – cultures that have developed separately through millinea. Car traffic along the street seemed less intense, less dense. Cars were distinctly fewer and, on average, older. The store windows were not filled. But the sidewalks along Nevsky Prospekt were full of walkers.

I thought I began to hear a chant in the distance – I could almost identify what it was but not quite. Odd. As we walked on down the boulevard, I kept hearing the chant through the crowd. Then I thought I saw way down the people-packed street sidewalk some walkers all in white. We were walking in their direction. Then I could hear it clearly: "Hare Krishna, Hare Krishna". A group of eight devotees all in white coming toward us. As they came by going in the other direction, we bowed to each other as they sang by.

We were approaching the beautiful Singer Building built about 1900, which planned to be the Russian national office for Singer; but, after the revolution, it eventually became a book and print store and was so when we came in. Quality wall prints of Tolstoi, Rachmaninoff, Marx, Dostoevski, and others. Rooms and stories of books shelf by shelf. I took a fine painting print of Tolstoy.

One kopek, please.

Rybachye turns bold

Our team, still creating, embraced the idea that, in Rybachye, an election had been recently held.

The team's drafting encompassed clearer descriptions of the values and priorities of each of the four teams and those of each team member. Our group discussions continued to become more focused. Four individuals would represent each team. Each individual's role would be sketched out; each role, written out, would take on character. (These were background papers, some for all players to read, some for only certain players. When it came time, in the game, each negotiator would play out his or her own role (improvisational acting is a term often used to describe this), acting out negotiations in meetings within each team and, when ready, negotiating between the teams in meetings they would hold together.

When one is participating on a team writing an improvisational drama, dreams, wild thoughts, and brain-storming are fair game for what may turn into valuable story lines to use.

So we began to imagine: (The following is from the Common Data Bank we were drafting: "An election was recently held in Rybachye which changed the composition of the [governing body]." The new multi-party coalition, joined by a Green group, took their places. "Approximately a month after the election, another major occurrence took place." Then what we had put together before: First, a young girl on a nature holiday with her father walked off for a moment by herself in the woods. She found a lovely, shiny vein of something, some kind of metal, in the ground, perhaps uncovered by the very unusual monsoon-like rains they had recently endured. She called her father over to see it. The vein glinted in the sun. Then the news began to come out. "Geologists from the Ministry of Industry [announced that they had] discovered a huge deposit of [high priority nationally needed] tin ore. This deposit is located to the northwest of Rybachye in an area between the Primorsky Natural Reserve and the wild taiga."

The Ministry, satisfied as to the vein of tin ore's significance, decided to mine it and build a refinement and processing plant on the site, then transferring the outcome to Vladivostok for distribution. "Green Earth, an environmental newsletter based in Vladivostok…, has called for an end to the 'wasteful destruction of the environment." The people of the area, including the indigenous peoples, become up in arms against the plan. The ecological conflict emerges with energy.

The team worked together on the fine-tuning, the further drafting of the play's descriptions and dynamics.

We flew home. The Russian and American teams corresponded for the coming year, refining the text, solidifying plans. Rybachye would rise in conflict the next year, exploring in the all-day simulation play the methods being learned that week for how to explore the solving of complex conflicts in a cooperative way. We considered the simulation play a more visceral level of learning.

Outside the full-size reproduction to scale of an old Tzarist palace (the original obliterated by Nazi bombers in World War II), nearing time for us to go home to America

At the end of our first stay in Leningrad, our team and the Russian team went together one afternoon to the faithful reproduction of a major castle of late Russian Monarchy located just outside Leningrad. The Russians had rebuilt it stone by stone after the Nazis in WW2 had blown it to bits.

Before we left the castle at the end of the afternoon, I was standing outside talking with Larisa of the Soviet team. We were speculating while our bus was warming up. How well would our peoples be working together 10,000 years from now? Perhaps if we and our heirs could all make it through the next turbulent periods between us and world-wide, perhaps people can have been easing our mutual problems together over time; and we as two proud peoples could come to know reasonable peace. Perhaps indeed. We must walk that way.

Together, we imagined the year 3000 A.D. coming in. We imagined it thriving. We imagined better and more sustainable policy for our long-future heirs.

Here it is now approaching dusk. As the sky grows darker, we climb again onto the warm bus, sit down together, and head back to the city.

Footnote: During our work there, and, then, based on NCA/CRI's teachings and the collaborative seminar curriculum that the exchange developed, leaders of the Russian team led the creation of the interdisciplinary academic field of "Conflictology" (a brand new term in Russian) first at Leningrad University (now St. Petersburg University.) The university developed an undergraduate and graduate program in Conflictology and began to talk about it with other senior institutions around Russia. Today, at least 25 Russian universities have grown undergraduate and graduate Conflictology academic programs exploring how to solve conflicts cooperatively.

Now Petr rides the horse of bronze

Dedicated to my hosts: Alexandr, Nina, and Masha
(Alexandr and Masha have now died.)

1.
Petr rides the horse of bronze.
Petr rides the sailing ship.
At dusk, the wedding couple climbs out
of the car and walks down along the river,
he in black, she in white. In this white night, when the sun barely
sets, he kisses her neck and throws a red flower down into the
water.

2.
At midnight in the Hermitage,
in the stillness, in the shadows,
Lorenzetto's body of a marble child
lies across a marble dolphin's
body's back. (From lost antiquity
comes the story of a child and dolphin
who come to love each other,
who came to play inseparably upon the water.
In a storm the boy's body falls and breaks upon
the ocean rocks. The dolphin comes and
desperately carries the body on his back to shore,
cannot revive him, stays up in the air,

cannot leave his playmate, dearest friend.
The dolphin stays in the air and dies,
his friend on his back, the two bodies
bathed in night.)

Two young lovers whisper to their
unborn child: We will not do with life
what Lorenzetto did in marble –
Nature the child; we the dolphin.

Rembrandt's old man, white hair
all in shadow, stares off the night-wrapped canvas
and out the window through infinite air.

"Petr the Great was always down there below
building boats with his men," the voice on
the Hermitage stairs said. "He was like that."

3.
The hermit awakens. She stands at the
window with the first of the sun. Her eyes watch
the little boats rise and fall, rise and fall
on the Neva waves, Across the water,
the vertical shaft above the glinting
bulbous dome points straight up at the sky.

4.
Now the main boulevard Nevsky Prospekt
is 250 years old. Huge bright baloons yellow, white,
and blue rise in the early evening City birthday air.
In 2003, Leningrad was 300. Will the Neva River run for a million?

5.
"It runs from Lake Ladoga to
the Gulf of Finland, to the Baltic Sea,"
Larisa said. "Very short but very wide."

She said: "Short, but full of water."
In the early evening frost, Alexandr Pushkin, 37, more than a century back in time, reaches up both his hands and runs them over the cold wood grain of his outside door, over the carved wooden flowers on it. His tears are growing cold. He hears the almost silent lapping at a little Moyka canal wave nearby and turns. The light
in the evening sky recedes so slowly that he doesn't even
see it go. He walks to the water's edge and watches
the sky in the little Moyka waves. He imagines himself
tomorrow, sees the woods ahead, and feels his walking
is a little slow. The flowers still mark the spot year around.

6.
In the Cathedral, sleek brown carved heads protrude
from the wall and frame. Their eyes
stare unblinking, blank in every direction.

7.
Katherine dreams of a flying horse.
The single huge stone sleeps.
The shovels do not exist.

8.
In the Leningrad early summer dawn,
light spreads across the sky.
On buildings very old and new,
shadows soften and dissolve.
In the light, nature is green; the Neva and
the sky are blue and reflect each other without error.
White clouds float like ships. Wedding couple,

Petr, hermit, Pushkin, dolphin, child
awaken and begin to rise.
In the trees along the riverbank,
young birds stretch their wings
and begin to sing.

9.
Yellow sunlight fills the Leningrad sky. There is
the visible Neva and the invisible Neva. Petr rides
the horse of bronze. High above the sea, Petr rides the sail.

The shield

1. August 19th
It had been just like with Jack Kennedy.
It had been just like with John Lennon,
just like with Bobbie Kennedy,
just like with Dr. King.

2.
Hours and hours in front of the
flashing TV screen, driving stunned
to and from work
with the news radio up loud.

3.
Coup d'Etat. Gorbachev, family
disappeared, likely murdered.
Reformist President Yeltsin surrounded by overwhelming

dictatorial armed forces. Hundreds of gray tanks moving
on in toward the center of Moscow. The Baltics
at gunpoint. Paratroops run forward with their
rifles toward big planes that whine.

4.
Last June, with my colleague Alexandr, I am riding down the
second escalator going further down below Leningrad's Nevsky
Prospekt Metro station. I see again on the wall coming up toward us from below, up towards us the massive gray and metal wall
sculpture moving closer on our right, a statue of 12th Century battle hero Alexandr Nevsky (Alexandr "of the Nevsky", of the Neva
River, the main river down from Lake Ladoga, heading toward
Finski Zalif (the Bay of Finland), flowing blue in waves,, curving

for aeons through town). In the sculpture, Nevsky's knights are a
human shield in straight line with him, all in heavy armor, all on
horseback, pausing at the ready, high up on this morning wall, all
of their eyes staring resolutely forward at their fate.

5.
It had been like when your precious glass
falls down through the air. In a moment, it will hit and
shatter all over the floor. You know that already,
can't move fast enough; and now it's the second before.

A few days later. I'm driving late Friday afternoon,
hot, North out of town, rush hour stop-and-go traffic
up Highway 80, heading for the North hills country
to write. Rolling hills green shapes increasing,

strong flickering sunshine on the dashboard
from which Russian poet Yevgeny Yevtushenko's voice
is booming out over the local National Public Radio station,
his new poem, "August 19", Yevtushenko declaiming it

in Russian, an announcer reading Yevtushenko's own
English version quietly in front. He's describing his climbing up
to be with his President, Boris Yeltzin, on the top step
outside in front of the Russian Republic's national legislative
headquarters.

They know that the coup d'etat's tanks may arrive against them at
any moment now. President Yeltzin speaks over a powerful micro-
phone to those tens of thousands assembled; then they are looking together out over the sky and this vast and growing crowd,

shoulder-to-shoulder, a growing human shield, red-yellow

flickering fires all around. I find I am crying as I drive.
Boris Yeltzin looks out over the crowd, then beyond that
out through the night over the barricades they are building.

7.
In the darkness, glints of yellow-red across this great shield in late
night bonfires. Still standing, still growing in every direction to the
tens of thousands, this shield glints gray-pink, then shades of pure
white with first dawn.

CHAPTER 2

Learning Conflict Resolution with Cuba
Through Action Research

Challenges to Co-Developing a Bi-Lateral Cultural
and Educational Exchange, Research Project, and
International Learning Community, 1994-1995, with the
Senior Graduate School of Diplomacy of the Foreign
Ministry of Cuba

From P. Kennedy's New York Times review of 1-15-12 on William Gibson's new book: "Thus as the world teetered on the edge of nuclear war in 1962, [Gibson] prepared himself for Armageddon."

Primarily in Fall **1994**, after tantalizing starts and stops and then with significant steps forward, we and Cuban counterparts worked on collaborative conflict resolution seminar planning together and then carrying our project out as a week-long full-time conflict resolution exchange/learning community, research project, and seminar in Havana. The full-week conflict resolution seminar, as things continued to develop, got stopped, changed, and moved forward again, hopefully to be ready to take place in Havana in spring **1995**.

From the U.S. side, conflict resolution professionals were under the aegis of Bill Lincoln, Executive Director of the Conflict Resolution, Research, & Resource Institute, Inc., Tacoma (CRI). On the Cuban side were primarily Cuban diplomats, professors, and senior graduate students in diplomatic training, and other international personnel, gathered under the aegis of the Instituto Superior de Relaciones Internacionales (ISRI), Havana, the senior diplomacy graduate school of the Foreign Ministry of Cuba. CRI later added co-sponsorship by the Institute for Multi-Track Diplomacy, Washington D.C. (IMTD)

Finally, I am setting this struggle down on paper. I'm reflecting on this adventure through the lens of my quiet retirement from consulting and university teaching of psychology and interdisciplinary synthesis.

Looking through the Cuban case file now, the whole venture comes strikingly back alive.

—∞∞—

These are the *beginning stanzas* of a poem I wrote in Havana during my first and second trips there to negotiate final planning for the project with my counterparts with ISRI. The **text** of the **full poem** is to be found at the very end of this chapter.)

Refugio

1.
February 1995. Havana.

I am walking down the narrow black
marble stairs at the Instituto Superior

de Relaciones Internacionales in Havana.

I have come alone for a series of meetings in final preparation for our planned seminar, exchange, research project, and learning community. The stairwell itself is old and dark, black marble flecked with gray. At each level that my Cuban counterpart Gabriel, and I go down, on the walls in front of us is a single stenciled black word in Spanish: "Refugio," along with a small black arrow pointing straight down.

2.

October 1962. Champaign-Urbana, Illinois

Holding our month-old son up on my shoulder, I am walking back and forth with him across our living room, our apartment across the street from the University of Illinois, where I am a student and where I have just bought the day's newspaper the front page of which shows on the coffee table, the headline:

> **"Cuban Missile Crisis:**
> **All Sides Threaten to**
> **Use Nukes Now!"**

I pace back and forth, holding my baby Jon to me, back and forth, holding his tiny warm body tight. His head lies on my shoulder, eyes fluttering closed. Our living room curtains are white with lace edges, now moving a little in a breeze. It's cool out. Twilight. The last light slowly leaves the sky. I hold my new son and imagine us and our tree-lined university town, without even time for a whimper, at the heat of the sun, all engulfed in flames.

3.

October 1962. Havana The same day

Gabriel tells me that he was holding up his newborn son, just four days old. Outside, Gabriel remembers, the officials are trying out the air raid sirens. The sirens wail up and down. Over and over. With absolutely new eyes, his son stares up into Gabriel's eyes, the world for him just begun. The new eyes blink. As it is becoming dusk outside, the practice sirens are still wailing. Inside, shadows draw across their room. Time for lamps.

(The full poem, "Refugio", appears at the end of this chapter.)

• How the plans for the exchange and research project came to be

Late August 1994, I was flying on Mexicana from Mexico City back up to San Francisco, having, over breakfast eggs and coffee, just decided in Mexico City with Bill Lincoln and Bruce Johnsen of CRI that I would negotiate for CRI (with Bill and Bruce's active participation) with the Cuban Government to see if we could co-develop a seminar/exchange/ learning community/research project to study interest-based, collaborative, and democratic negotiation together, and with the seminar to take place in Havana.

In **early 1992**, in Washington D.C., Bill Lincoln, Executive Director of CRI, had initially met with Alfonso Fraga, then Chief of the Cuban Interests Section of the Swiss Embassy (essentially Cuba's Ambassador to the U. S., during the U. S. bar against diplomatic relations), (Formally, the U.S had dropped formal diplomatic contact with Cuba 50 years ago.) Lincoln and Fraga established that a collaborative conflict resolution seminar should be tried. On **July 1, 1993**, in Washington, Bill Lincoln and retired U.S. Ambassador John McDonald, President of the Institute for Multi-Track Diplomacy (IMTD), met with Mr. Fraga, as John McDonald put it, to further consider "the subject of an educational-cultural project in Cuba, one which would focus on conflict resolution skill-building." After this, John McDonald and Susan Levin had two follow-up meetings with the Cuban "Ambassador".

———∞∞∞———

As I watched out my airplane window, down on the ground way below me vast shapes of green, brown, and blue shared the land mass; I thought of how the U.S. and Cuba are, no matter how we consider it, not only separate and autonomous national entities, but also are joined inexorably in one small geographic neighborhood. Neighborhoods always work better in a state of durable peace.

I thought of the profound estrangement, rancor, and the almost catastrophic Cuban Missile Crisis in the early 1960s between our two countries (taken to the very very edge of nuclear war) and how this ongoing polarization was not inevitable and need not, indeed must not, be permanent.

The benefits of normalization and cooperation between our countries are compelling. Learning more from each other on how to understand and resolve conflict could be part of a start. We need to work together to, finally, leave the Cuban Missile Crisis completely behind.

Daniel Ellsberg about U.S. world thermonuclear weapon targeting change done by the **early 1960**'s:

"...but **between 1955 and 1960,** (the U.S.) retooled (our Atomic weapons). We modernized. We put in Teller's bombs, H-bombs – same plans to hit the same cities – and the (projected) casualties [worldwide] went from 20 million to 600 million, first strike; and, sort of, nobody noticed."

The Cuban Missile Crisis was then our most direct and ravaging experience of being brought right to the edge of thermonuclear war, one that could have savaged Cuba, the U.S., the Soviet Union, and, perhaps, could have descended into the danger of "nuclear winter" widening across the world.

Ellsburg asks: "How does it feel to be in a plane with two rival teams of hijackers?"

———❧———

To get perspective, we need to go back about 500 years. Spain conquers the island of Cuba. They rule it until 1900, with a growing civil resistance over the last many of those years. Around 1900, Spain was driven to war with the United States, which took Cuba's side, only to begin swallowing Cuba up as soon as Spain had been driven out.

(Actually, the United States has eyed Cuba since U.S. Revolutionary War times. It was seen as a potential U.S. colony. John Quincy Adams is said to have commented to Thomas Jefferson that Cuba was becoming "a ripe apple to be picked.")

At the beginning of the last half-century, Castro and his peasant army overthrew the cruel despot Fugente Batista. Once the Cuban government gave up trying to negotiate with the U.S. and instead negotiated with the Soviet Union, the U.S. began treating Cuba as a pariah. The U.S. formally severed formal diplomatic relations with Cuba back then.

To add to the perspective, the U.S. then tried over many years to kill Cuba's President, Fidel Castro. And then once, in the late fall of 1962, the U.S., Cuba, and the Soviet Union came, trippingly, to the very brink of a catastrophic thermonuclear war. Noone who was an awake adult then has entirely recovered from that. But never again. Now, in this new atmosphere, we can learn dialogue with each other now.

Aware of history in the past U.S.-Cuba relationship, aware of how the U.S. has used force, aware of having been carpet-baggers, aware of how dangerous our mutual alienation grew in the Cuban Missile Crisis and after, this chapter describes an approach to problem-prevention and early conflict amelioration which we specifically used in our own bi-lateral organizational planning process with the representatives of the Cuban government and diplomatic culture. We sought to make our experience working and learning together succeed. Could our dialogue do any good?

If you wish, you can look at this work as an informal case study. Our aim was to creatively prepare, together with our Cuban counterparts, a strong Havana learning community seminar week together. We just hoped we could bring it about, in spite of all the things standing in our way, sometimes seeming impenetrable. To help us increase our chances, we decided to apply our own conflict prevention and early intervention methods, which we had practiced for years in our work in the U.S. and in other countries.

In advance, we sought to anticipate and then study carefully a number of expected key initial problems – ones that we would need to solve together. Early on in our planning, we would try to find, in advance, potential problems that would need to be resolved as they emerged over time among the project bi-lateral decision-making areas. This we coordinated with the development and carrying out date/report/act entries onto our master calendar.

The idea was that we could try to catch and ameliorate potential planning conflicts in advance - to do early intervention to reach out to upcoming organizational development conflicts before they emerged or grew out of proportion. The barriers to pulling this off were so substantial that we needed an advantage, which this process could help.

As much as possible, we wanted nothing to threaten the success of our pre-planning for the collaborative cross-cultural seminar we wanted to bring about. We thought one benefit of this "front loading" of our anticipatory thinking responsibility would be to help get research and planning done ahead of time, to develop options, before and in preparation for the key decision-making deadlines we would have to meet.

(You might call this goodwill "anticipatory diligence". It also could be communicated with the Cubans. We could signal to the them our larger good will and determination. Most fundamentally, this method increased the slim chances that we would be able to get approval for, plan for, and actually hold this exchange.) Stay tuned.

—∞∞∞—

Bill, Bruce, and I knew this would inevitably become such a very hard case to bring to fruition. There were too many barriers. The U.S. had long-since put in place a very strong travel ban between the U.S. and Cuba. Our countries had already continued a Latin Cold War for decades.

I kept thinking about how we had most narrowly averted a thermonuclear war against each other, one which, according to some scenarios, could have almost mechanically expanded itself to engulf the world.

The U.S. had been blockading Cuba for a half-century. Now, finally, decades late but deeply appreciated, nonetheless, the current Administration has negotiated renewed diplomatic relations with Cuba, the two capitals have reopened Embassies, and our U.S. President headed for Havana to reopen our Embassy and our relations.

In Washington, the "Cuban Interest Section" was an organization under the aegis of the Swiss Embassy (the only "official" Cuban representation in Washington until most recently). Even within this, at the time we tried to develop our "research project", official U.S. diplomats were on absolute orders that they could only talk to Cuban counterparts (1) about the Havana-to-Florida boat people problem and, later, (2) about interdicting the international drug trade. The U.S. diplomats were explicitly forbidden to talk with their Cuban counterparts about anything else.

Technically, as we at CRI developed our plans, our team was in dialogue with a government with which the U.S. was officially in this large conflict. We hoped that we could win an official research project designation from the U.S. Department of the Treasury, a status which was known at that time to be very, very unlikely, very hard to come by, nigh unto impossible. (Although understanding that it was almost impossible <some said it absolutely couldn't be done), obtaining such an official "research program" designation would be about the only way we could work in Cuba "appropriately".)

Incredibly, the gulf between countries was so absolute that in 1994, as we began this stage of the venture, no workable international telephone system was then in operation between the two countries. (A major storm had destroyed the Cuban phone system, and apparently the U.S. had blocked outside people from going in to fix it.)

Over and over, the U.S. emphasis had been on **no contact** combined with strong hostility and threats of financial penalties or prison.

On top of this, our two organizations (CRI and ISRI) had no history whatsoever of working together in the past. Literally and figuratively, we spoke different languages.

The list of difficulties in our trying to bring about the seminar/ dialogue on democratic negotiation went on and on; but we decided, nonetheless, to give it a serious try. We thought that such a peaceful, respectful conflict-resolution study and communication exchange deserved to be done, could be valuable to hold and to learn from, for us as well as for the Cubans.

So we started forward, in spite of it all. Who and what would we find behind this Latin Iron Curtain which our government had erected around Cuba? The following is what we found.

Obispo Street

1.

In old Havana, seven Laurel trees line a small shady square at the foot of Obispo Street. I stand here on a Friday morning. For many years past, this old Havana square on Saturday afternoons held poetry readings and novel readings, writers reading out loud to their hearers gathered under the hot sun.

2.

Across the square, head erect,
one thin old woman stands
in an old light blue cotton dress
behind a table lined with books,
her right hand leaning on
the table's squared edge.
Another woman, younger,
sits behind the table, arranging
each book as if it were a flower.

3.

Around the square, old buildings display lace-like black wrought iron banisters around their second floor. In the center of the square stands a bronze statue of Don Francisco de Albear. He is holding a marble book in his marble left hand and a marble pen in his right.

4.

The brass marker says: "In November 1887, he invented the canals through which the waters of Havana run."

On war
Sun Tzu
(About 500 B.C.):

"The best method is not to need to fight at all."

⟨∞⟩

By October 1994, after many calls with Bill and Bruce and then with the Cuban Interest Section of the Swiss Embassy, our negotiation with the Cubans began to move forward. The Cuban representative agreed to plan a meeting together in Washington, D.C., to consider jointly building a research project peace and conflict resolution seminar. The meeting was to take place in Washington, D.C., at the offices of the Swiss Embassy's Cuban Interest Section (the old Cuban Embassy).

After more phone consultations with Bill and Bruce, on behalf of CRI, I flew to Washington to hold a first, exploratory meeting with Cuba's representative to these talks, Dr. Oscar Garcia, Rector of the Instituto Senior de Relaciones Internacionales (ISRI), Havana (the Foreign Ministry's senior diplomatic graduate school); potentially, they would be the Cuban host institution at the Cuban Foreign Ministry). Dr. Garcia flew in from Havana. Over the years, Dr. Garcia had been a practicing physician, then Cuba's Ambassador to Spain and head of Cuba's delegation to UNESCO, and then the head of Havana University. In Havana, now he was the head of ISRI.

Besides Dr. Garcia and I, joining us in the meeting were to be retired U.S. Ambassador John McDonald (IMTD), Washington, D.C., plus Cuba's Third Secretary of Academic Affairs, Rafael Noriega.

We walked toward the front entrance to the old marble Cuban Embassy (at that time literally the "Swiss Embassy Cuban Interest Section", since Cuba couldn't have an Embassy here). Once inside the ornate entrance, we were immediately ushered up a winding white marble staircase to the upstairs and there led to an ornate, elegant sitting room, complete with lovely crystal chandeliers. An aide brought in very strong excellent Cuban coffee in small white china cups. They were kind. When the four of us had settled in and agreed on our meeting agenda, we began to go over together potential outlines of what could emerge, a one-week-long full-time exchange between U.S. and Cuban participants centered in deepening and enlarging our understandings of each other and of how to build trustworthy models of conflict resolution together.

In the meeting, as we were working through the agenda subject by subject, we could see that their interest in trying to do this together was increasing. We were finding together some good correspondences in approaches, some important shared values.

Then in the middle of the meeting, Dr. Garcia asked me: "In this training, can we talk together about what we wish?"

(We at CRI had talked such a question through carefully, knowing that official U.S. diplomats could not yet do this – they could only discuss boat people and, later on, collaborating on drug smuggling intervention. Fortunately, in fact, we definitely wanted to collaboratively design the curriculum with them; and the subject matter for our conflict resolution exchange/seminar/research project was entirely open.)

Yes, we assured him, subjects for dialogue that week were definitely open; and we wanted to design the week and its subjects *together.*

Dr. Garcia's smile widened. Then his face took on a look of delight. I found myself becoming happy in turn and smiled back. I began to sense that we all would indeed try to do this joint adventure, to do it together. We were becoming ready to give it our best try.

Precisely, the central question for the meeting was to be whether the two sides could seriously consider combining a U.S.-based conflict resolution team and a Cuban Foreign Ministry team - through the Foreign Ministry's ISRI) - to jointly develop and hold in Havana a full-time, week-long dialogue on collaborative conflict resolution. It was imagined to be an exchange between about nine participants on a CRI team and, on an ISRI team about 30 members of the Cuban diplomatic corps, diplomats, international specialists from other Ministries, international relations graduate school professors and senior students.

Our exchange could possibly provide one place where citizens of both countries could openly explore their perceptions of the other's alienating ways, consider the dynamics together of how conflict gets exacerbated, and focus together on alternative ways of finding common ground and collaborating in resolution of conflicts and learning to work positively building joint projects.

In these talks, if we could pull this off, a main focus would be on designing the week to encourage extensive facilitated open dialogue between the American and Cuban teams and to work on exploring methods for collaborative, cooperative interest-based democratic negotiation).

We shook hands. Smiles all around.

Dr. Garcia headed back to Havana to begin the exploration. (Over the next few weeks, Dr. Garcia took the concept through the proper agencies and departments in Havana. Then Cuba's Foreign Minister agreed.

This American-Cuban project was suddenly on the verge of taking on a life of its own.

———⊷———

Joanna Macy, <u>Dharma and Development</u>
"Development, to be effective, must merge with the indigenous ethos and interact with the specific genius of a culture."

———⊷———

Naturally, as we began to move forward, we wanted to have as little friction generating as we could manage with our Cuban colleagues. We wanted to focus our growing energy and momentum, especially, on our positive cooperative seminar-planning – improving our plans for the exchange and making more systematic arrangements for carrying the plans out with focused and practiced energy. We were becoming aware of the start of trying, in spite of the odds, to plan to win it together – to go, one by one, through the calendar months of preparation together ahead, step by step by step, looking for ways to jump-start planning for each stage. We began settling in to our joint task.

Not many natural models to use for developing such an international learning community. (We came to tap resources through Evergreen State College, Olympia.) So as we went forward, we developed our own model. Its essence was mutual respect combined with cooperative development, aimed toward developing and holding a bi-lateral community of learners exploring cooperative (interest-based) conflict resolution.

In early conference calls, Bill, Bruce, and I developed a good systematic way of working with our own (CRI) internal planning and decision-making process. We wanted to model our own methods to work smoothly when inevitable inner-team differences and problems came up. We wanted to pull the venture off, in spite of the long odds. We wanted to increase the odds of success any good way we could.

• Seeking U.S. and Cuban Government approval

Early on, we at CRI began developing the written applications materials that would be necessary for official consideration by the U.S. Department of the Treasury, consideration of this venture as an official U.S. "research project". We needed their ok, though that might prove to be impossible. The Department had been given the task for approving exceptions (if any) to the U.S. travel ban. (We checked their materials through internally, then with advisors, then with legal counsel. Soon, nice and early, we sent the stack of completed application materials off to Treasury requesting their ok for our Havana seminar project. We wanted them to have plenty of time before we needed to know.

On paper, we proposed what was beginning to develop into the structure of a strong bi-lateral educational exchange and research project, organized as an intercultural and bi-lingual learning community for that week together. We checked in regularly on the applications. Little to no response from Treasury. We continued to wait. And then call. Meanwhile, we were learning that, on the Cuban side, their travel Visa Department was the key body we needed to put paperwork through in Cuba. As soon as we knew what Cuban institution would be the one we should seek permission from for our project, we began to request their paperwork for us to fill out for them. As soon as we received them, we filled them out, and sent them back. Being early was part of our plan.

We continued to study the legal environment of our case with an expert attorney whom we had gotten through a small foundation grant. We realized that all the way through this, we would have to step very, very lightly and carefully, mindful of the regulatory climate both here in the Treasury Department and in Cuba.

• Continually soliciting issues that needed consideration

All project-long, for almost a year, we kept asking ourselves and each other what were the central and key subsidiary questions that we needed to prepare soon or now. For our master calendar, when did each issue/question need to be answered for sure. This information development process came to be used, then, on both sides, on a continuing basis, sometimes emerging as joint master calendar planning. This continuing search revealed, in advance, a number of potential areas of conflict almost ready to emerge, things we could work on and try to ameliorate now, so they wouldn't slow us down later. Emerging problems could often be worked with before they hit. (Managing the project, I continued to ask for questions from those others on both sides in leadership and decision-making positions and then passed the results around.)

We kept trying to see <u>what questions would emerge</u> in each of several categories. An old adage suggests that the better you can plan your work, the better you can work your plan. Through the nine months the priority questions that needed priority answers generally emerged (with encouragement) from these categories and could often be anticipated in advance by mentally walking through the logically and illogically necessary development stages and actions to be done – things that would have to take place and each within certain (and sometimes implacable) time frames). By having each main category established and developing, questions to work on continued to emerge and stimulate the work on them well before deadlines would actually start to intrude. The more done early, the less stress. The less stress, the wider the opportunities for full functioning in the project.

The less often and less intense the time pressure on the parties, the better. The less time pressure, the more time for the issue's ramifications to deepen and ripen naturally into view in the mind. Ideas, building blocks, solutions began to emerge with time. (Still, much had to be finished inside tight time constraints. Some time pressures were built in. Some appeared mid-route. Some matters were able to get good inner-team and bi-lateral development time, very careful consideration. The key.)

As the bi-lateral exchange planning continued to develop, a number of categories held important issues and questions. Sometimes, for instance, considering a particular issue would give rise to another issue which, although we had not had it in active consideration, would have to be settled, in fact, before the issue we were directly looking at could be finally settled. (Alternatively, had we had not fully engaged with the time limits and concept development needs of the advance planning and carrying-out process, the project would have been so very more vulnerable to the potential ravages of the unexpected, the emergencies, the continuing experience of Murphy's law.)

Also, by keeping one's eye on a "critical path" toward the goal, one could help minimize the need to subsequently have to take things back, remodel them again, and re-fit them into the whole plan (a bad move for time, money, and morale) to make them work.

Murphy's Law: "If anything can go wrong, it will."

An apparent corollary: "Decisions Tend to Require Completion Before Enough is Known". This being true suggests even further the importance of anticipating possible troubles and taking action together to solve problems before they start or soon after they begin to emerge when you catch them. Think of it as preventive and ameliorative action.

The February 1994 trip

By December 1994 and January 1995, we knew that we had an agreement with ISRI and the Cuban government. We would put on the seminar in April, if all things worked out. We still had not heard anything definitive from Washington about our U.S. permission. Cuba, through Dr. Garcia, made it clear in writing that they were preparing to move ahead with us to finish joint planning and hold the conflict resolution seminar/exchange.

Bill, Bruce and I decided that I would travel to Havana in late February 1995 to complete plans with ISRI and to spend time at the exchange site to discuss logistics and finalize curriculum with our Cuban colleagues.

So I found myself one midday in the big, shiny, loud, bustling Mexico City airport, standing at the Cubana airline counter.

On the flight to Havana that late February day, I thought through again and again the approval complexity we were in the midst of.

The consulting attorney had made it clear that only if the Cubans paid for our way entirely once we were in Cuba could we declare a different kind of exception to what we were doing - getting written approval as an official research project from Treasury. (The key was that the statute says specifically that it is not that you cannot GO to Cuba, it's that you cannot spend a penny there for any reason. If you did, you would be subject to severe U.S. fines and penalties. If CRI, any funders, or U.S. participants contributed to the trip's cost, which almost had to be the case since Cuba was basically broke, then to be ok we must get the Treasury's blessing. But if Cuba would pay for the expense (from goodness knows where), we thought we would have protection from the Treasury travel ban exception process altogether.

I knew I was taking the risk that if I couldn't get the Cubans to pay everything for our trip, we still were waiting, hoping for the Treasury approval to come and come in time. And in the meantime I was making an as-yet-unauthorized trip. What if neither of our approval methods worked? What should we do?

Thus, of course, I was concerned. But at the same time I was now sitting listening to the Spanish all around me, sliding into my first experience of Havana and of the Cuban government.

After a good flight and smooth landing, I emerged from the plane into the hot Havana air. Beautiful new airport. My counterpart, ISRI's Dr. Gabriel Perez Tarau, who I'd never seen before, met me with a car outside. We got in back. His driver was cordial in Spanish. It was hot in the car too, but we let breezes in and we were in motion, headed for ISRI at the Foreign Ministry. Big heroic posters of Che along with posters of Fidel were everywhere along our route as well as posters delivering government exhortations – on health, prevention, and politics. On the road we were driving along, cars were almost all 1959 or older American cars. Mostly Fords, Chevys, Mercurys, even DeSotos. Since 1959, the U.S. had blockaded against any more U.S. cars going there at all. (A number of shiny new Japanese cars were entering the mix now.)

Almost everything was dusty as we drove, the dwellings generally older and in increasing needs of repair. As we drove along though, I began to see beauty. Architectural forms. People, seeming to be friendly with each other and proud. The city slow-moving. In "La Habana Vieja", the beautiful oldest part of Havana, is a working/business district. I found building after building, street after street, showing an amazing 1820's architecture, a combination of old Spanish and very early Victorian combined into a unique hybrid building form. (The U.N. has designated this area as a "World Heritage Site". I found that it is being refurbished block after block to its old glory under an ingenious plan which draws grants and international investments to rehabilitate the buildings and then rents out the beautiful restored historic buildings to provide rental income which in turn can pay to rehabilitate the next block, etc.)

For my stay, we drove first to the place I was going to stay, a rather simple but clean bed and breakfast on an architecturally interesting street within walking distance of ISRI. For civility, the first day, I began there to try out my fragmentary Spanish which I had been learning on tapes in the last months of preparation.

In the early afternoon, after I had done some unpacking, I went to meet with Dr. Garcia at his office in ISRI. Much of the way I was walking next to the quietly rolling ocean.

In Dr. Garcia's office, we greeted each other heartily and got right to work. Soon we had agreed on meeting agenda We started talking together. Because the matter was so important to me, I raised with him our need to see if the Cuban Government could consider covering our U.S. team costs, because only that way could we be released from the travel ban and the consideration of rare exceptions from the U.S. Treasury. At that point, Treasury was continuing to say they were considering our application - now long on file with them. We were asking as a long shot that we be considered an official exchange and research project. Our concern was that the people at Treasury would either say no (which they were reputed to be doing all the time) or would not act in time for us to go.

Dr. Garcia suddenly looked sad. He sat silent for some time. Then he said: "Would this be a deal-breaker"? (He was asking whether we would pull out of the project if Cuba said no to our funding request.)

"No," I said. (Bill, Bruce, and I had tried to talk this through back in the U.S.) "No. This is not a potential deal-breaker. We're committed to this project. We intend to come here to Havana to have our exchange week together at ISRI, in Havana, regardless of whether you and the Foreign Minister can find any funding." (Because of the way the travel ban legislation had been written, their funding the program, if they could, their funding would help protect us in another way from U.S. government banning the seminar.

I knew I had to keep in mind that, since the Soviet collapse in the early 1990's, and with it the end of the huge monthly subsidy and oil payments from the Soviets to the Cubans (the oil payment had been huge), the Cubans had become so poor that when they had lost their Soviet petroleum allocation, they had decided, out of necessity, to resort to ancient farming methods. They began using oxen again almost exclusively to pull their farming equipment to bring in the crops to feed their people. They were that kind of broke.

Dr. Garcia said he would take our request to Cuba's Foreign Minister that evening. He said he hoped he'd be ready to talk to me again about it the next morning.

We met again in the morning. Our plan was to go through our agenda and then go to look over and review the seminar site, the classroom configuration, and finalize seminar learning plans.

Dr. Garcia opened the morning meeting with his sincere apologies. First, he said that they really did want us to come and would work actively with us to prepare to make the week together really productive. Still, the Foreign Ministry had had to decide, he said, after a careful discussion, that they just could not possibly afford to cover our costs. (This meant, with that possibility gone, we would have to try to get Treasury's ok for us as an official research project, after all.) But he emphasized that they wanted very much for us to come. And I said we would carry through.

Hot weather all the time, even at night. That night near midnight, I lay on my bed, hot, with covers thrown off, sweating heavily, in the pitch dark, worrying and trying to figure a way through to a safe journey. I was afraid Treasury might end up saying no to letting us go to Cuba. What then? I felt deeply committed to the success of this project and the bi-lateral dialogue across such antique polarization. It must heal. Laying there, I felt so hot and exhausted. And since I had not secured a financial commitment from the Cubans (which I honestly hadn't really expected they could manage to afford – but I had had to try the idea and hope), I felt myself in such a strange and ambiguous position: In Havana, without U.S. approval, with our application with Treasury still only pending. Planning a unique meeting of cultures. I felt a little like Alice falling down the rabbit hole.

Lying hot and sweating in bed, sheets now wet too, in the dark I watched up hanging from my ceiling, the slow-turning blades of a fan – my eyes looking at a last image turning as I fell asleep.

As I fell deeper into slumber, I could just vaguely make out a thought through the growing fog inside my head: Somehow, this really needed to be done. It deserved to be done, whether or not we finally got an ok from U.S. Treasury. This might help improve safety and understanding. The fog inside was becoming complete. We must do this, no matter what.

The last push
As always, the program had so many last-minute details. Phone calls, e-mails, itineraries, making calendars for a dozen U.S. participants continue to move toward fitting together in anticipation for the work for a whole team week overseas.

And as the days went on, we still got no Treasury Department approval. We called but it seemed to do no good.

Finally, a few days before we were planning to leave for Mexico City, we finally hit the brick wall. It was time for a final decision to go or not go in the absence of a Treasury Department approval for an exception to the U.S.-Cuba travel ban.

We polled the U.S. participants. They decided to go ahead, no matter what. They signed onto the final travel plan. Retired U.S. Ambassador McDonald "agreed…as a former diplomat, to defy the rules and go anyway."

Near the last minute, the Cuban Visas arrived.

On the day we were scheduled to fly to Mexico City to reconnoiter at a designated hotel near the Mexico City Airport, the team one by one from their various airports rose into the air and headed for Mexico.

I had my final bag packed. I was dressed ready to go out the door. I put my bags by the front door.

Just a few minutes before I was going to walk out the door and drive to the San Francisco Airport, my phone rang. I answered on the third ring. A voice said: "Would you please go to your FAX machine?"

Out from the machine's rollers came a FAXed document – our team's acceptance by the U.S. Treasury Department as a research project eligible for our exception from the U.S.-Cuba travel ban. We were ok to go.

❧

Coming in from the Mexico City Airport nearby, our team met for dinner and a coordination meeting in the hotel. We cheered as we passed out copies of the new Treasury Department ruling and each person's Cuban entrance Visa. The meeting was boisterous and then it became quiet. We shared ideas and plans for a few minutes. We wished each other a good rest.

And then, in the morning, we found ourselves high in the air, flying to Havana.

The Exchange

Nine experienced conflict resolution practitioners and teachers from the U.S. Thirty eight Cuban participants, government officials primarily from the Cuban Foreign Ministry but including participants from five different Ministries in the Cuban Government, plus senior professors from ISRI, and a handful of their best senior graduate students in Diplomacy.

During the week seminar in Havana, the CRI-ISRI-IMTD learning community reciprocated lectures, did small group and one-to-one work together, participated together in long expertly facilitated dialogues across our cultures, and did negotiation simulations. Video recorded the events.

Note on study methodology: During the week, the study used primarily qualitative methods and generated theoretical options, explored case study material, studied as well as experienced negotiation simulations and considered possible new ones, collected narrative/anecdotal data, and engaged in a wide variety of dialogic inquiries, as well as reviewing basic epistemological assumptions and methods. A Likert Scale in Spanish tested participant satisfactions.

At the opening meeting Monday morning April 3rd

Bill Lincoln opened his comments with thoughts on what happens when we speak:

"The first ingredient in a negotiation definition is to deal with proper communication. Is it noise? Are people really hearing what we're saying, in terms of fact, and in terms of the emotional context about it? Are we really sending a message that is full, that is complete, that is comprehensive, not only in fact, but tells truly where we're coming from in terms of our spirit, our hopes, our fears?" (1995, p. 19)

Dr. Garcia opened his comments with this: "We talk about the differences in US-Cuba [relations] considering the last 35 years [in 1995, he was speaking as starting from 1960], and that is part of the reality of the history; but it is not the total history. The problem is … difficult, as it is a problem of 150 years, and must be understood also. That has to be realized (by) the United States, the government, and the people. There are things that have happened in the last 150 years in relations between Cuba and the U.S.A. (that are) necessary to understand….We must sit without conditions and…talk of everything – maybe…talk first about the things that are easier and then go to the more difficult ones…. We have to begin to do it."

The week of dialogue began, at first with some hesitancy, some distrust, then increasingly with growing trust and strengthening dialogue. Here is the outline of study:

Monday, April 3

Working definition of conflict, conflict behavior, nature of conflict – Cuban perspective, Cuban/U.S. teams in dialogue

Tuesday, April 4

Interests/Issues, six needs (guest speaker), Cuban/U.S. negotiations – Cuban perspectives, Cuban/U.S. teams in dialogue, negotiation exercise, conflict assessment, Cuban/U.S. teams in dialogue, what needs to be negotiated – Cuban perspectives, Cuban/U.S. teams in dialogue

Wednesday, April 5

Position and proposal development, negotiation exercise, Cuban/U.S. teams in dialogue, human needs/psychology in conflict resolution (from reptilian brain to pre-frontal lobes/transpersonal actualization), multi-track negotiation, Cuban/U.S. teams in dialogue

Thursday, April 6

Obstacles to settlement of disputes, methods of overcoming obstacles to settlement, Cuban/U.S. teams in dialogue, procedural/substantive/psychological satisfactions, Cuban/U.S. teams in dialogue, preparation for main negotiation simulation for Friday

Friday, April 7

Main negotiation simulation, Cuban/U.S. teams in dialogue, characteristics of capable diplomats, closing, overall assessment of the whole week's course of study. (The assessment was done entirely in Spanish.)

In addition to our daily seminars, we met with such public officials as Cuba's Foreign Minister, the Cuban Parliament's International Affairs Commission (the equivalent of our Senate Foreign Relations Committee). We were graciously received and spent intense meetings talking in English and in Spanish. We also talked about arts issues with the National Writers Union.

We were taken out for our getting to experience more about Cuba to such places as the Bodagita del Medio, where some of us, John McDonald notes, sat at a table where Ernest Hemingway had written "The Old Man and the Sea".

We saw the Cuban National Art Museum.

One late afternoon out swimming in the ocean, I noticed an older guy floating by on his back. It turned out he was a U.N. executive; and for years, he told me, he had been spending all his vacation time in Havana. "Once the U.S. drops the Cuban travel ban, masses of people will flood in here and the Cuba we know will be ruined."

I spent hours walking along the ocean sea wall, the Malecon, watching the walkers, the singers, the lovers, the waves.

Each day of the exchange, I asked Cuban participants to score their assessment of "the pertinence" and "quality" of each period during our week together in Havana.

As the exchange became more and more positive, we began wondering: If we could succeed together with them for that week, it seemed we were developing one good trust-building model that worked, at least one example for the two cultures, locked in a fifty year old Latin "Cold War" fight.

It turned out to be realistic and exciting to stop and successfully study collaborative peace-making together. Each participant during the week explored ways which might eventually become measures of aid in the evolving search for common ground upon which we can build an equitable and long-lasting peace.

At the end of the week, when asked about the total week's "quality of learning environment" they scored the week 98.82%. When asked about the week's "pertinence to their life and work", they scored the week 99.38%.

Last day, just as we were departing from Havana, John "asked the participants which country in the world is their favorite. Every single one said 'the U.S.'."

An exchange Cuban participant said to us on the last day, Friday, April 8th: "For me, the more important matter, the very, very good experience, the wonderful work, really was that you, all of you, came to Cuba as friends, as brothers [and sisters] and spent five days with us to give to us an idea how to work – what we can do. At the end, what I can pick up is, indeed, if we have a good will, we will find a way out, a possibility to talk and to understand each other."

Retired U.S. Ambassador John McDonald:

"This is the first time, in my experience, and the Cubans verify this, that a team such as ours has been to Cuba. So it is historic."

A U.S. participant:

[In the past] "the United States and Cuba [have been] very much partners in a dysfunctional conflict. [Potentially] each is a partner the other is looking for – not only for a resolution to the conflict but [also to build] the working relationship that we're supposed to have."

A Cuban participant:

"We had opposing viewpoints. [We found] a common viewing point, so, physically, instead of being this way, we began to look at the problem together, collectively and collaboratively, solving the problem. We owned the problem together, and I think that was a major shift."

A Cuban participant:

"Wouldn't it be wonderful if "conflict resolution" became another language of the world, if everybody had the same language and before they resorted to force and violence and treachery to resolve disputes – would say, wait, there's another way to do this. Let's sit down. Let's see if we can negotiate this and have your interests and my interests somehow be satisfied."

Refugio
(The complete poem)

1.
February 1995. Havana

I am walking down the narrow black
marble stairs at the Instituto Superior
de Relaciones Internacionales in Havana.
I have come alone for a series of preparatory
meetings. The stairwell itself is old and dark,
black marble flecked with gray. At each level Gabriel, my Cuban
counterpart, and I go down, on the walls in front of us is a single
stenciled black word in Spanish:
"Refugio," along with a small black arrow
pointing straight down.

2.
October 1962. Champaign-Urbana, Illinois

Holding our month-old son up on my shoulder,
I am walking back and forth with him
across our living room, our apartment next to
the University of Illinois, where I am a student and
where I have just bought a newspaper the front page of which lies
on the coffee table, the headline blaring:

Cuban Missile Crisis: All Sides Threaten to Use Nukes Now!

I pace back and forth, holding my baby Jon to me,
back and forth, holding his tiny warm body tight.
His head lies on my shoulder, eyes fluttering closed.
Our living room curtains are white with lace edges,
now moving a little in the cool twilight breeze.

The light is slowly leaving the sky. I hold my new son
and imagine us and our tree-lined university town,
at the heat of the sun, without even a whimper,
all engulfed in flames.

3.
October 1962. Havana - The same day

Gabriel is holding up his newborn son, just four days old. Outside,
the officials are trying out the air raid sirens. The sirens wail, crying
up and down. With absolutely new eyes, his son stares up silently into
Gabriel's eyes, the world for him just begun. The new eyes blink. It
is becoming dusk, the shadows lengthening across the room.

4.
April 21, 1995, Rohnert Park

"So this senior Russian general, who had been in charge of nuclear weapons on Cuba at that time, turns to them..."

I'm back from the Cuban exchange. I've just read an amazing
New York Times article, and my dear friend and I are driving
down the Expressway; I'm describing what the article said - that
there had been meetings last year and this of former top Russian,
Cuban, and American policy people from the time of the Cuban
Missile Crisis, in which meetings they have been exploring with
each other, right now - for the sake of history - what really was going on behind the scenes by each side during the worsening of the
crisis, perhaps our nearest brush with unloosing a thermonuclear
World War III.

"So this senior Russian General, who had been in Cuba then, turns
to them in response to a question.

(The question posed by Robert McNamera, U.S. Secretary of Defense then, had been: "Of course, if attacked, you would have sought instructions from Moscow... Right?")

- The Russian General turns to him and says "Oh, no. I was not going to contact Moscow at all. I had nuclear missiles which were fully operational. They were clearly at my command. They were all pinpointed on U.S. targets. And, if attacked, I would have immediately given orders to fire them all."

McNamera, now white hair on his head, is sitting across the table from the General. His mouth drops open. He is silent, turns ashen. Silence. In almost a whisper, he says to them all: "I had no idea," he says. "I had no idea."

5.
Havana. February 1995

"What does 'Refugio' mean, Gabriel?" I ask, as we sit down on the old gray couch in Dr. Garcia's waiting room.
"Well," Gabriel begins, "the signs are old. It's
about a long time ago." He looks down and pauses.
Some birds are singing in the trees outside the window.
"During the Missile Crisis, in October '62, these signs went up here to remind us, if the sirens went off or we were bombed, to go down the stairs to the basement,
as a shelter, as a refuge."

"Of course," he stares long out the window, "if your country had dropped on us atomic bombs, the basement refuge wouldn't have helped at all, but it might have withstood conventional weapons."
Gabriel and I were quiet together. The birds outside rustled and

flew up out of the tree. Their songs echoed. If we in the U.S. were hit with atomic weapons, I remembered, our newspapers had talked of immediate nuclear retaliation.

6.
Over Mexico. April 10, 1995 - on the way back home

I pause, put my pen down, and walk up the airplane's thin aisle and get more black coffee up front. The coffee pot is carefully held in place by strong curved metal holders. The exchange is all over. I want to get back to my loved ones. I stop in the aisle, coffee in my hand, and take in how now I have loved ones in Havana too. Two children squeal for a moment and are quiet. We are flying at 35,000 feet. I walk back toward my seat. Two adolescents are asleep. Brown faces, white faces, black faces, sitting next to each other in rows, quiet, reading, dozing, staring out the windows at the strange afternoon-lit world below. One baby sobs for a moment and puts her head on her mother's shoulder and is quiet again. This plane's jet engines make a dull high hiss as we fly. Outside I can see below us mountaintops touched with snow.

7.
Havana. April 6, 1995.

On Thursday afternoon, the exchange had been almost over.

The week has obviously been very good indeed. It had worked out.

Gabriel and I are sitting downstairs. We are both smiling. We've just been negotiating something and have agreed and we are done. Above us, a ceiling fan revolves slowly, slowly. Through the slatted windows, afternoon light is slanting in. It is very warm, and green palm tree branches are waving in the afternoon breeze. We are quiet. "You know, even that week in Fall 1962," Gabriel says, "even that week, even then, we were so alive. Cubans have a kind of joy of life. We call it "agria." Cubans feel the present with such great intensity. Even then...," he says, and stops. He looks intently, silently down at the floor.

I find tears are running down my cheeks. I try to say something to him and find I can't. The ceiling fan slowly turns and turns. Outside, high in a palm tree in the courtyard, a brightly multicolored bird is singing a long song, then repeats it. It echoes in our room. We hear a broad roar of laughter coming down from our colleagues upstairs, the buoyant laughter rolling down the stairs. The whole group upstairs is laughing and clapping. The light slanting in makes sections of the floor before us stripes of a bright white. I watch the light beginning to fall. I feel the breeze across my face. Gabriel is silently staring out the window. My breath is quiet. We sit there. I hear the turning, turning of the fan.

CHAPTER 3

Transparency in Collaborative Negotiation
About Basic Human Needs

Especially A Contrast of Two Negotiation Styles
and their Relationship to Dr. Sidney Jourard's
Concept of Transparency

(| n 1999, a much-condensed version of this manuscript became
a chapter in **Invitations to Dialogue – The Legacy of Sidney
Jourard**, Kendall-Hunt Publishers). This essay was also award-
ed the Saybrook Graduate School and Research Center Peace
Essay Prize 1998-1999.

— ⟨∞⟩ —

**"The crisis of our time is not shortage of food, space and
energy; it is the failure of dialogue...The learned incapacity
to hear and understand what another human being is saying
and the choice to respond in dishonesty is at the heart of
our dilemma on the shrinking planet we call Earth."**

Sidney Jourard, **Journal of Humanistic Psychology,**
Vol. 18, No 1, 1978, p. 47

Table of Contents

Summary and Introduction

We read and hear about negotiation every day–negotiations among countries, among members of legislatures, among businesses, even, if we think about it, within and among families, including our own. In fact, we ourselves no doubt perform some form of negotiation almost every day. As Roger Fisher and William Ury (1981, p. xi) put it, "Like Moliere's Monsieur Jourdain, who was delighted to learn that he had been speaking prose all his life, people negotiate even when they don't think of themselves as doing so." Thus, the study of negotiation is practical as well as theoretical. In addition to helping us analyze what we read in the papers and better understand the workings of our legislators, our decision to improve our understanding of humane (or, alternatively, tragic) negotiations may have important implications for our satisfaction with the conduct of our own lives.

The negotiation process as it is practiced professionally is going through a number of transformations. Adversarial approaches have been the most common forms of negotiation in the U.S. Although adversarial negotiation is a strong method, a number of problems with this traditional method have pointed toward the value of developing more humanistic forms of negotiation. These are now emerging. This writing explores the problems with certain of the effects of the traditional methods (such as lack of effective listening, distortions of perception, polarization, distortions of truth, and exacerbated conflict aftermath). It then turns to a discussion of issues contained in a principal emergent negotiation form, i.e., collaborative basic human needs/interest-based bargaining or negotiation. Sidney Jourard's concept of transparency, developed to apply to personal lives, also appears directly applicable to clarifying our understandings of why, how, and what this newer, more cooperative form of negotiation can accomplish in both the public forum and in our personal integrity.

In adversarial negotiation, the form of professional negotiation that has been the predominant tradition in the U.S. and the West, negotiator opaqueness has been prized. "Poker playing" is often used as an analogy. The assumption has been that if the "opponent" knew what one and one's side really wanted, beyond the current "position" the negotiator is showing on the bargaining table, the opponent would use this knowledge to undercut one's negotiation needs, potentially leading one's team to being cornered and one's positions "injured," one's mind hurt and regressed. The negotiators fear they would then "lose" and "lose face." They concentrate on the chess-like movements they make, one move after another. Unfortunately, Fisher observes, "as more attention is paid to positions, less attention is devoted to meeting the underlying concerns of the parties. Agreement becomes less likely." (Fisher & Ury, 1981, p. 5)

In the hardest negotiations, in the past, one can say that a Social Darwinian survival-of-the-fittest mentality has often prevailed. A zero-sum game mentality assumes that for our side to gain something, we will have to take away from the other side an equal amount. Being secretive, our job would also be to keep the opponent guessing about what we would do and what we really want, not letting the opponent in on our real strategy. We would think we were increasing our team's chances of getting the most for our side (and allowing the least to the other side) by the end of negotiations. Unfortunately, as Fisher and Ury see it: "arguing over positions endangers an ongoing relationship – Positional bargaining becomes a contest of will. Each negotiator asserts what he will and won't do. The task of jointly devising an acceptable potential solution tends to become a battle. Each side tries through sheer will power to force the other to change its position....Bitter feelings generated by one such encounter may last a lifetime." (pp. 5-7)

In the light of these and other limitations to the traditional approach, another style of negotiation has emerged from early work by Harvard teachers and practitioners of negotiation in what was to become the critically acclaimed Harvard Negotiation Project, and in its conscious and unconscious application of such concepts as Abraham Maslow's hierarchy of human needs (Maslow, 1961) into a matrix for understanding need sources of conflict. (Many now believe that such a hierarchy of human needs needs to be at the core of study and action on a foundation of striving to satisfy the basic human needs of the parties in conflict.)

The author writes from the vantage point of over 30 years of collaborative conflict resolution work, including ten recent years as a principal of a small conflict resolution consulting group and as teacher in a number of international teaching engagements with Bill Lincoln's Conflict Resolution Institute, Tacoma, including project co-managing and teaching in an educational and cultural exchange and research project (approved as a research project by the U.S. Treasury Department and by the Cuban Foreign Ministry) between nine U.S. conflict resolution experts and 30 Cubans diplomats, Foreign Ministry officials, senior professors) under the auspices of the senior institute of the Cuban Foreign Ministry (ISRI) which trains Cuba's foreign service professionals & other officials in such related fields as international trade. (At a number of points, this paper makes reference to that exchange.)

The author's writing here refers to this emerging method of negotiation by three of its perhaps most common names, collaborative negotiation, basic human needs negotiation, and interest-based negotiation, which this writing will combine into "collaborative negotiation of basic human needs". With useful variations and emphases, this general method goes by an even wider number of names (such names as "collaborative negotiation," "collaborative human needs negotiation," "basic-human-needs negotiation," "interest-based negotiation," "principled negotiation," "win-win negotiation," and "transformed negotiation" (in which last case the new methods are seen to change and improve the whole foundation and gravitational flow of what negotiations can accomplish within the organization over time). In these methods, the negotiators (or negotiating teams) know that it is ethically correct, psychologically sound, and <u>to their own advantage</u> to seek to understand and reasonably satisfy the interests and needs of the other side(s), the other parties, <u>as well as</u> those of one's own side.

This necessitates dialogue to try to find out what each side "needs" in the outcome. Each side can learn more of what each party's highest priorities are. While transparency is not employed in the adversarial model, it is of the essence in the collaborative model. In fact, the more successful the transparent acts on the parts of the collaborating negotiators working for the opposite sides are, the better and more satisfying the proposals for settlement will be.

It is in this intersection (considering both technique and the potential for contributing to healing) that implications of Sidney Jourard's work on the value of transparency become most apparent and compelling. Given the real circumstances of each negotiation, if the parties involved seek to learn enough of what each party most needs and wants, if the parties strive (judiciously, using common sense, and based on growing trust) to tell the opposite side's negotiators what they most need and want in the negotiations – and inquiring the same about that opposite side's key needs and wants – and if the parties then strive to incorporate these top-priority understandings into the proposals leading to the outcome agreement, they will significantly increase the likelihood that the settlement will be reached and implemented and that it will be mutually equitable and satisfying enough to each party that the settlement can and will endure.

Adversarial Negotiation

Turkish Proverb:
"A weapon is an enemy even to its owner."

This chapter seeks to walk a careful line to avoid stereotyping or oversimplifying adversarial negotiation. It is a strong method. Many have no doubt used the method over time with distinction, skill, and even with a certain empathy. But there are some common negative consequences of the method which occur so often as to have stimulated the emergence of alternative forms of dispute resolution, including collaborative basic human needs, interest-based negotiation. The second half of this chapter will focus on its potential. But the chapter begins by reviewing some of the methods and especially problems of the primary traditional negotiation method, **adversarial negotiation**.

(Note: As dissatisfaction with adversarial negotiation has grown, new light has also been falling on traditional Native American conflict resolution methods, likely the oldest traditional methods on this continent. While adequate discussion of these methods is beyond the scope of this writing, the author recognizes that (a) any discussion of "traditional" U.S. method is actually incomplete without them -and (b) they are fascinating and fully deserving of more study and presentation in their own right.) (See LeResche, 1993.)

Furthermore, brain thinking discoveries using fMRI technology bring us toward a substantial deepening of our understanding of some facets which appear to be "wired".

Social Darwinism

In his studies in the 19th century, Charles Darwin came to believe that, over the millenia, those members of species whose characteristics were most appropriate to the ecological niche they occupied, and who were also more flexible and adaptive as those environments changed, would fare best in passing their genes on to future generations.) He believed that this principle applied to whole species, as well. Those that fit best or adapted best to fit niches and needs had the best chances to create viable offspring having passed on to them characteristics most useful for the future. This process came to be known as "survival of the fittest." In later decades, social commentators began to apply this principle to the human social actions sphere. This became known as "social Darwinism," in which circumstances a kind of "dog-eat-dog" mentality was prized, with the presumption that the "fittest" would survive the competition, then breed and leave its offspring better for the future. This, such theories claimed, was as it "should be".

Looking at this from the perspective of negotiations, you can see how the application of this principle could lead the more dominant group to insist upon getting its own way, maximizing its own advantages, denigrating any needs and rights of anyone else, and unambivalently enforcing its self-enhancing outcomes. Forms of Social Darwinism (pre-Darwin, before the name was used, and post-Darwin) have informed the development of negotiation theory and method.

As a point of departure, Lewis Cozer (1964) defined "social conflict...(as)...a struggle over values and claims to scarce status, power and resources in which the aims of the opponents are to neutralize, injure, or eliminate their rivals". (p. 8)

Some negotiations bear clear claw marks of this approach even today.

"Gesellschaft" and Buber's "I-It"

Sociology has a German term, "gesellschaft," in which people are identified and valued by their place "in the division of labor and nothing else". (McWilliams, Jr., 1962, p. 76) This concept is counterposed to, the opposite of, "gemeinschaft," defined by McWilliams as "an association of persons based upon intimate knowledge, direct contact, a day to day sharing of life, of common traditions and aspirations, of a sense that there abides a bond written in nature itself between the [persons] of that community". In this contrast, negotiations using only "gesellschaft" as the basis for relations among the disputing parties could have one party uncaring whether the other party fares well or ill. Look at now.

Theologian Martin Buber (1937) understood humans as being of absolute value in their own natures. He saw each person as holy and deserving of appropriate treatment as a bearer of that utter value. He saw human transactions as of two fundamental kinds. The first kind of human transaction he called "I-It," which occurs when one human "uses" another, when one does something to/ with another human in which he/she treats the other person as a "thing," not as another holy person at all. When this takes place, when another is treated as a "thing," one does not sense it necessary to look out for the other's welfare. The other is there to be used and used up and, as expedient, to be thrown away. The "I-It" approach is of the sort that one might use if one is approaching a human transaction from a Social Darwinist point of view. How would it feel?

In the worst circumstances, with a low, nominal, or non-existent valuing of the other person or the other party to the conflict, the negotiation can smash ahead. As Schaller (1966) puts it, "conflict is the clash of differing points of view. A century ago ... theorists used the word conflict to describe the violent clash of irreconcilable interests, loyalties, values or opinions." (p. 73)

Conflict and adversarial methods of bargaining

William Lincoln (1995) describes adversarial bargaining as "relationships and behaviors when one or more disputants actively oppose others in a hostile manner in order to achieve specific results; uncooperative in most unpleasant ways; to be contrary in volatile ways." (p. xvi)

In adversarial negotiation, one usually focuses on one's position, the list of outcomes one is insisting his/her side must take from the negotiation. In the adversarial negotiation model, the negotiator seeks to win for his/her side everything possible from the list of positions one puts on the bargaining table. As necessary or "advisable," these wins are to be at the expense of the opponent's side. (Some adversarially inclined negotiation advocates even take the technique to the point of seeking to symbolically "destroy" the other side.)

Winners and Losers

Adversarial bargaining assumes that one and only one side wins. In this view, one side winning defines the other side as losing. The process of bargaining is seen as a chess game, in which the symbols are organized around the rules that, in the end of the game, one lives and is triumphant; the other is vanquished and is set to die or recede into the background. This win/lose balance is also called a "zero sum game" the mathematics of which always shows that one side gains to the degree the other side loses – in each transaction and transfer.

Some Problems with Adversarial Negotiations

Thus far, this chapter has briefly reviewed general problems. Now the paper will review several specific problems which often arise from the heat (and regression) of adversarial negotiations. To a certain degree, problems in communication are endemic to humans as a species; but adversarial bargaining, with its emphasis on an "us-vs.-them" mentality, seems to exacerbate certain communication problems. Among them are five to be considered here: Non-listening, polarization, distortion of perceptions, concealing of self, and dishonesty. Let us start with the adversarial propensity to not listen.

Non-Listening

From Jourard's point of view, "the learned incapacity to hear and understand what another human being is saying... is (a key to) the heart of our dilemma on the shrinking planet we call home." Note that Jourard studiously uses the word "learned" in this comment. The problems being discussed here are not just inherent in the human organism; we may have predispositions, but the problems are made manifest as outgrowths of confrontations involved in adversarial negotiation. We learn alienating habits, which then become part of a negative self-reinforcing feedback loop.

Roger Fisher and William Ury (1981) observe that "angry people often fail to hear what others have to say. And whatever they hear, they are likely to put the worst possible interpretation on both the words and actions of someone who is seen as an adversity." (p. 24) Furthermore, anyone who has spent much time at the bargaining table understands what Jourard (1995) means when he describes much of contemporary communication as like the 'parallel play' of two-year-old children, or like the professors in Stringfellow Barr's 1958 novel who, when together socially, lecture past one another alternatively and sometimes simultaneously." (p. 68)

Polarization

Jourard wanted people and organizations to explore more transparency not only for the good it can do, but also because its absence can cause dysfunctional dynamics to grow, interlace, and become more complex to deal with and more complex to unravel. Not listening combined with the anger that arises in adversarial negotiation abets a number of problems, one of which is unnecessary and unwarranted polarization.

Fisher and Ury observe as ubiquitous that "In taking positions, we tend to assume that an adversary's interests and ours are directly opposed." (p. 36) This assumption is very common. It is most often quite wrong. But the misperception that it is true can stimulate the creation of positions and actions in negotiation that are anywhere from ineffective to utterly tragic. This is the case, whether it occurs in an individual family or on the world stage. Charles Webel (1996) concludes that "...splitting self and others into irreconcilable and antagonistic poles is both infantile and pathological. It degrades and sometimes demonizes other nations and societies, many of which have cultures and histories at least as varied and complex as our own." (p. 19)

In Faces of the Enemy, Sam Keen (1986) shows that once we polarize, we seem to dehumanize those at the other pole. This dynamic is particularly important because it can lead to perception distortions which can lead, in turn, to the most monstrous consequences, such as massacre and war. How does this work?

Perception distortion

Most of us presume that our perception is objective and neutral. Yet Miles' Law (Bloch, 1980) states that "Where you stand depends on where you sit." (p. 44) Our perceptions are often vitally dependent upon our past experience and our current position and role. Put another way, Fisher quotes a Russian saying that "everyone looks at the world from the belltower of his own village." Even if true, why should this matter?

Fisher and Ury explain that "we often handle conflict poorly because we are each prisoners of our own thinking....We tend to collect evidence that supports our prior views and to dismiss or ignore non-conforming data. This screening process has at least three levels: We selectively remember what we want to; we selectively recall what we remember; and we revise our memories to fit our preferences. The more we become convinced of our views, the more we filter out information that would lead us to question them." (p. 21-22)

Jourard recognized, in Tomson's (1996) words, that "human beings are subject to self-delusion and bias of every kind. Communication between individuals can suffer from unintended distortions or interferences, originating either from the source, en route, or upon reception." (p. 33)

Negotiation is complicated enough, in and of itself. In adversarial negotiation, the rising tensions among the parties complicates negotiation much further. The complications brought by these first two complex levels are themselves compounded when, as may happen, the very nature of the realities being dealt with begins to come into question.

Beginning this perceptual exploration shows us that, if we are going to broaden our understanding of how the positive negotiation methods discussed in the second half of this chapter can help, and if we are going to appreciate the importance of Jourard's contribution, we first have to delve deeper into the workings of the negative complications of adversarial negotiations. This will set the stage.

Habitual concealer of self

Tomson's (1996) review of literature potentially relevant to Jourard's concept of transparency cited findings by Pennebaker. When Tomson reviewed Pennebaker's studies on the communication of difficult, anxious, and traumatic material (Pennebaker & Breall, 1986; Pennebaker, Hughes, & OHeeron, 1987; Pennebaker 1993; reviewed in Tomson, 1996), he found a revelation "that the capacity to confide appears to be stunted in a remarkably high percentage of people, whatever their age, class, or ethnic background." (p. 19) For Pennebaker, "... story after story revealed deceit, tragedy, and misery."

Finally, reviewing Jourard on this point, Tomson's wrote "that a large part of our misconceptions are due to the fact that man is a habitual concealer of himself. As a result, our concepts and beliefs about human behavior are organized around mistaken images of our needs and capacities." (p. 2)

Dishonesty

From the self-cloaking arises a dishonesty which has both outer and inner implications and ramifications.

As an example of outer implications which can confound attempts at negotiation, consider the compounding confusion possibilities of a corollary to Murphy's Law (Bloch, 1980) called Lieberman's Law: **"Everyone lies, but it doesn't matter because**

nobody listens." (p. 75) This phenomenon can bring ludicrous distortions into the bargaining process.

In addition, and even more serious, Tomson notes that "it is important to clarify that the unhealthy consequences associated with deception include self-deception." This can bring surreal distortions into the bargaining process.

Jourard has said: "In a society which pits man against man, as in a poker game, people do keep a poker face; they wear a mask and let no one know what they are up to." Now we see that in the poker-like situation which Jourard has described, the poker players can all too easily turn their own respective internal maps awry.

In his survey of pertinent research, Tomson found that W. F. Fisher (1985) has proposed the following three interrelated necessary conditions in which the possibility of self-deception arises.

The first condition is conceptualized as evidenced when one is already committed to a particular understanding of some phenomenon of one's world (i.e. its meaning has already been posited). The second condition is that certain emerging significations of the understanding render that concept (meaning) ambiguously uncertain (our model is threatened). The third condition is that one experiences anxiety as a result of one's already posited understanding being challenged. In summary, the possibility of deceiving oneself arises when one is faced with a possible transformation of one's world as one already understands it, and one experiences anxiety as a result. In other words, when an individual is confronted with information that doesn't conform to the individual's model of reality [the person] experience(s) anxiety as a consequence.

To add to the distortions, according to Fisher, all acts of self-deception are characterized by two meanings.

> They are: 1) that one turns away from the possibility of taking up and exploring one's anxiety, thereby preventing it from informing, and 2) that one denies and/or explains away the ambiguity, thereby rigidly reaffirming their previous understanding. Being self-deceptive is an effort to avoid/refuse those personal truths which would conflict with or render ambiguously uncertain other truths to which one is already committed. In essence, to deceive oneself is not to keep oneself from explicitly knowing what one already implicitly knows; it is to refuse to discover that which might undermine our preconceived notions. To be self-deceptive is to sustain an unchanging sense of one's relations to others and to the world; it is to reassert rigidly that one already knows who one has been, is and/or can become (i.e. it is an effort to maintain stability)....We tell a kind of lie about ourselves, a lie of selective perception. (pp. 35-37)

Using the term "behavioral duplicity", Cameron and Magaret (1951) postulate that as children, we learn, in Tomson's words, "to withhold certain disclosures because of the associated painful consequences to which they lead." We learn, most likely in accordance with the laws of reinforcement, to present a censored version of our real self to others, a phenomenon Jourard (1958) termed the "public self."

To Horney (1958), we run the danger of mistaking this image for our true self. This can happen if we forget that we are playing a game of controlling our self-disclosures in a manner to affect how others understand us. We can get so busy with this that we literally forget who we really are.

By alienating and distorting communications and truth at the negotiation table, the adversarial negotiator stands the distinct chance of rationalizing himself/herself into a kind of self-alienated and alienated-from-truth illness which further poisons the negotiation table atmosphere and makes resolution on healthy procedural, psychological, and substantive terms all the more unlikely.

Looking at the phenomenon from an explicitly psychological point of view, Tomson says that

> a number of theorists have noted that being dishonest with oneself and with others (inauthenticity) is at the root of both neurotic and schizophrenic functioning (Anonymous, 1958, p. 58; Jourard, 1964, p. 64; Kaiser, 1965, p. 65).

In Tomson's view (1996), in each case,

> behavioral duplicity is hypothesized as both necessary and sufficient for the existence of neurotic disturbance. Behavioral duplicity can thus be considered both a symptom and a means for achieving neurotic functioning (p. 59).

Now we can begin to see a lengthening chain of confusions and disorientations leading from an origin point (an adversarial negotiation stance with its emphasis on negotiator opacity) through non-listening, polarization, perceptual distortions, self-concealing, and dishonesty – each link in the chain making resolution of the conflict harder.

Generally unintended negative effects on negotiation
Viewed from this perspective, the alienations and self-alienations made more likely by the chemistry of adversarial bargaining can

make negotiation an unnecessarily and even absurdly complicated and confusing experience, one which can seriously erode the optimal functioning of the organizations (families, businesses, governments) for which the negotiations are intended to serve a stabilizing, planning, and even community-building role.

The negotiator and the observer of negotiation may ask how the negative links of chain are likely to affect the negotiations which operate as adversarial enterprises: After some agreement is completed, what is the likelihood that parties will remain angry and search for and interpret loopholes? What is the likelihood of one side continuing to "bad-mouth" the other side? What is the possibility of renewed litigation, appeals, escalation of conflict? What other kinds of conflict aftermath may occur? Note that within complex organizations, a variety of other negotiations might be taking place simultaneously or within months of the negotiation being examined. The unhappy resolution of this conflict can adversely affect other negotiations, even when the other negotiations have nothing directly to do with this particular problem or case. Group morale, dedication to the "company" goals, individual and group illnesses, multicultural communications – all can be affected.

The effects of what we've been considering can bring sadness, major losses in human resources and human solidarity potential, and tragedy. Groups can ignore crucial realities containing a compelling need for working together in common. We can remember the old story of four people in a rowboat, two at either end, with the boat in utter distress in a storm. One end of the boat is sinking deeper and deeper into the ocean waves, with water gushing in, flooding that end of the boat. The two people at the lower end are bailing water like crazy. At the other end of the boat, momentarily riding high up out of the water as the other end sinks, one person at the high end turns to the other and says: "It's a good thing we're not at that end!"

In fact, it appears that Jensen's Law (Bloch, 1990) applies to situations where adversarial bargaining has set off the chain of negativities I have just reviewed. Jensen's Law states: "Win or Lose, You Lose." (p. 192)

The adversarial method itself appears inherently flawed.
Johnsen (1996) thinks that it takes maintenance of reasonable adult maturity to consider a method of negotiation that has the capacity to lessen or reverse the chain of negatives outlined in this paper's first half.

To consider a collaborative approach requires us to begin to reverse in our minds the adversarial methods to which we have previously been exposed.

Dealing with Recalcitrance
Before this chapter focuses on collaborative, interest-based negotiation, here follows a note on dealing with those who do not open up to your offer of cooperative negotiation. Hopefully, most of one's negotiations can be with those open to collaboration. But sometimes (as is true with most of life), one may have difficulties, may have to deal with those who are "closed" and combative. In this position, one can remember that not everything can or should be negotiated. Sometimes parties in conflict can't agree on how to describe the problem. Sometimes the issue is right and clear but the timing is wrong; it's not time yet for the parties to enter dialogue, negotiate, and try to settle.

Sometimes, in spite of the problems created by adversarial negotiation methods, and in spite of the values of collaborative negotiation methods, one may find oneself needing to negotiate with a bargaining party or parties who choose to be negative, at least in the early stages. The adversarial approach may be practiced by the other side(s) in spite of one's appeal to find ways to study together to collaboratively solve the dispute at hand. This insistence by the other party on adversarial methods may arise from the other side's lack of experience with collaborative dispute resolution methods. (Or lack of successful experience.) The other side may have become at least temporarily too polarized or alienated as a result of the negative side-effects of earlier adversarial negotiation between the parties. The other party may be working from another developmental or operating stage that does not seem to fit with collaboration. Just as one example, an adversary may be working partly from the reptilian level of the human brain, a phenomenon not unusual when the party feels danger, significantly inhibits trust-making, assuming the other is an implacable foe.

Faced with an adversarially oriented opponent, one may move into a mode of negotiation containing both adversarial and collaborative characteristics, offering both "carrot and stick." In collaborative negotiation, one seeks to understand one's opponent's needs and interests. This study is doubly necessary when one is faced with an antagonistic opponent. By coming to understand the opponent, one seeks to learn what will deeply motivate.

One can say: It is my preference to deal with you collaboratively. However, if I haven't gotten your agreement yet to work collaboratively, and if I can't get it soon, I may find it necessary and in my interest to escalate the conflict until we have your attention and you decide and work out with us how to study this problem collaboratively, after all (Townsend, 1998).   Lincoln (in Towsend & Robinson, 1998) defines 15 dispute-resolution strategies. The later ones, if necessary, grow increasingly militant. Lincoln's twelveth listed strategy, for instance, is "direct action," which outlines depriving the opponent of "its work force,... its market,...critical electoral support,...favorable public opinion and support."

One can say: I don't want to do this. I want to work collaboratively with you. I want us to develop a settlement that will protect the interests of both of us and thoroughly. I will work on this if you will. If you start as being unwilling to work collaboratively, I will work on advancing my interests while studying and possibly acting on yours. When you change your mind, we will work together. (Townsend, 1998)

If one's analysis of opponent interest has been accurate and deep, a sudden interest in collaboration may emerge from the opposition, after all.

To start preparing ourselves for thinking about a collaborative method, let us remember that military genius Sun Tzu (1988) told his readers well over 2000 years ago, at the beginning of his still widely read book <u>The Art of War</u> : "The best method is not to need to fight at all."

Collaborative Interest-Based Negotiation
(As an introductory caveat, please note that Bruce Johnsen (1966) asks: "How many people have the introspection capability to know whether they are being transparent or not? It seems that a medium

to high level of maturity and self-knowledge is a necessary baseline for even considering this kind of approach.")

In the Glossary section of <u>In Pursuit of Promises: The Practitioner's Course in Collaborative Negotiations and Cooperative Problem Solving</u>, Lincoln (1995) provides his short definition of a more functional process of negotiation:

> ...a complex yet manageable process (composed) of three primary sub-processes - proper communication, effective education, and the responsible utilization of power – intended to prevent, manage, and resolve dysfunctional conflict via interest satisfaction as provided in the development, exchange and maintenance of promises (p. xxi).

Partners we've been seeking

In <u>The Transparent Self</u>, Jourard (1964) provides a key starting point for differentiating collaborative interest-based negotiation from adversarial negotiation. Whereas adversarial negotiation seeks to be opaque, collaborative negotiation seeks to work together to find mutually fulfilling solutions. Jourard says: "I think it is almost self-evident that you cannot ... behave toward (another person) so as to foster his happiness and growth, unless you know what he needs. And you cannot know what he needs unless he tells you." (p. 3) In collaborative interest-based (basic human needs) negotiation, the negotiator actively seeks to know the other side's interests, the other side's most essential wants and needs, and to make the negotiator's own side's priority interests known to the opposite side, as well. Honest communication of priorities and, overall, an attitude seeking and providing more transparency plays an indispensable role.

Each side seeks through dialogue and confidence-building activities to develop sufficient trust for the other side(s). As this trust develops, it becomes possible for negotiators increasingly to disclose key interests which must be taken into account to develop a deep mutually satisfactory proposal for settlement. Knowledge of each other's perceived key interests gives each negotiator a much more realistic opportunity to conceptualize and develop proposals for settlement. These will contain provisions which will have been designed in good faith to try to satisfy the key interests and needs of both the negotiator's side and the opposite side - within a realistic overall formula which incorporates all parties' priority interests/needs.

On a practical work level of putting this into practice, Lincoln points a second level of positive function out to us when he states that "the opposing disputant (can become) the partner for whom we are looking to join us..." In this partnership, he advocates "... making and keeping promises which will resolve the conflict in an equitable, practical, and durable settlement agreement." (p. 88)

Over the years, in my own consulting practice, working with parties who often come to me in the midst of destructive negotiation fights, sometimes in strike, I find myself facilitating those parties learning how to redefine and streamline their necessary working relationships with one another. Each party can then move away from seeing the other side as "enemy to be taken from and torn down." Ideally, each party comes increasingly to see the interests of all the sides in the dispute and the negotiators on all the sides as potential collaborators, potentially searching by teamwork for answers to problems in common, answers which satisfy needs.

It is understandable that people accustomed to adversarial negotiations, ones unfamiliar with collaborative interest-based negotiations (or without trust in it), would be skeptical of this approach. For instance, as Jourard stated (1978), referring to cases with individuals: "One who never has known dialogue–only deception, duplicity, and cunning–believes that a person who is open, and invites others to be open, is crazy!" (p. 49)

Collaboration based on basic human needs and interests
Wide-ranging successful experience described in such books as the best-seller, <u>Getting to Yes</u> (Fisher & Ury, 1981), is suggesting that collaborative interest-based bargaining has much to offer the person who is frustrated with the problems generated under the old system, as previously discussed in the first section of this chapter. These persons often want to explore more collaborative approaches to find common ground. Using a collaborative interest-based method looking at human needs often makes it possible for each party to walk away from the negotiation table, in the end, as a "winner."

The balance of this chapter considers collaboration based on the parties' interests and needs, listening, talking, understanding, looking at paradox, existence between the poles of arguments, transparency, satisfaction, and approaches which can emerge. It ends offering some preliminary speculations on this approach to negotiation being pertinent to the 21st century.

Bill Lincoln (1990) taps the chalk board insistently. He is showing students how he insisted that opposition negotiators pay attention to his client's key human needs and interests, which he had listed on the board in that negotiation. "Everything you say," Bill repeated for the class what he had previously said to the other side's negotiators, "everything you say and propose I and my team will look at by evaluating whether or not your proposals meet my client's key interests that I've put up on this board. If your proposal meets these listed key priority interests which we have, we will pay attention and study what you've done and try to work with you to resolve our conflict. If your proposal doesn't meet my client's key interests listed here on the board, you can be sure that we will reject your proposal on the spot and act accordingly."

In Lincoln's view, specific basic human needs and interests contain crucial principles, values, belief systems, those which "need" to be satisfied if the conflict before the parties is to be equitably, practically, legally, and durably resolved.

(Note: For simplicity's sake in these pages, I use the term "interests" to also represent "basic human needs".)

In the process of the negotiations, these interests can also be categorized by whether they are procedural needs, substantive needs, and/or psychological needs. In most struggles, all three levels of interests are involved. That is to say, negotiators and their clients must first agree upon the negotiation procedures to be used. Clients need these procedures to be implemented, as agreed, in an equitable and pragmatic fashion. Clients need to feel that the substance of what they are negotiating is being treated with respect and worked into the proposed resolution.

This fair treatment in both content and process will help them develop psychological, substantive and emotional satisfaction with the way the negotiation has been conducted. It is also helpful for people to think of interests in terms of those outlined in Abraham Maslow's hierarchy of human needs (1968). Lincoln explains it: "Interests for each person are simply manifestations of these basic needs ... (as they) become the driving forces for that person's behavior. Interests are WHY a person acts–or doesn't act–in any particular way at a particular time." (pp. 82-84)

As one becomes more conscious of the dynamics and substance of the negotiations of which one is a part, one can increasingly look for those interests and issues which one and one's opponent have in common. In addition, one may be able to identify those which, while different, can be provided for in a complimentary fashion. As Fisher, Kipelman and Schneider (1994) put it,

> in looking behind the other side's positions, we will first be looking for interests which we and they may share. Both passengers in a lifeboat want to get to shore and may subordinate their differences in pursuit of that common purpose. But we will also be looking for areas where their interests differ from ours. Upon examining their respective interests, passengers in a lifeboat may discover that one prefers bread and one prefers cheese, leading to a prompt and amicable division of the rations. (p. 38)

Seeking out the other party's interests in a negotiation can lead down particularly useful paths. One more example is in looking deep inside the opponent's statements, studying them for underlying, implicit interests which may be driving that party's approach to the negotiations. Fisher and Ury (1981) advocate reversing roles in one's mind to try to empathize with how the other side is thinking and feeling. "Role reversal and the other techniques discussed above not only help us understand another's point of view, they help us find room to maneuver by illuminating needs and concerns that lie below the surface." (p. 46) Lincoln adds that "effective negotiators often prepare a chart that compares the elements of their proposals with the other side's interests, and then try to test the other side's receptivity to proposals before they are

even offered. Areas of overlap will serve as areas for possible compromise...." (p. 202)

Interest-based dialogue opens up negotiations. Whether negotiations are occurring in the family, the workplace, or internationally, negotiators can learn to be more candid and revealing in
their communications with the other side(s). Lincoln encourages
negotiators to "learn why an offer is being made or resisted...for
such will always be related to interest satisfaction or interest dissatisfaction." Transparency enables the parties to learn each others'
priorities and thus prepares them to figure out how to incorporate
each other's primary needs in fashioning solutions. Such solutions have a better chance of being accepted with the resultant
agreement having a better chance of being durable. (p. 208)

By growing candor based on growing trust, we can learn: "that
no durable settlement agreement is possible unless significant self-
interests for all disputants are satisfied at acceptable levels – all
things considered." (Lincoln, 1995, p. 210)

Listening

A common saying among traditional negotiators (most especially
attorneys) is that they have two gears, talking and reloading. Any
"listening" which occurs may be primarily to see whether the other
side is listening, capitulating, stalling, or fighting back.

Jourard (1978) could sense how important the listening process could be to developing trust and transparency. To understand the other, we must listen. Jourard said, "while education is
not only listening, listening is a necessary part of it...It is no small
thing really to listen, because we listen, not just with our ears,
but with our entire being—our imaginations, our memories, our

feelings, our bodies. Really listening means stopping the random noise with which we silently occupy ourselves. What we hear said to us can be a matter of life and death." (p. 50)

Listening and what we can discover by listening can make all the difference, even in situations of great importance. Jourard says that "when we trust someone enough to listen to them, we derigidify our model of the world. Familiar talk concretizes, or "sets," our model of what the world is like, while new language, if we hear it, remodels our image of the world as a sculptor shapes clay into new images. The greatness of Freud, of Sullivan, of Rogers, is the greatness of a great listener! They hung in and really listened to, heard, and understood people to whom their colleagues would not listen....I hear the person, and I attempt to make my imaginary model of reality correspond with his or her sensory reality." (p. 51)

> Socrates: "The unexamined life is not worth living."
> Ram Dass: " The quieter you become, the more you can hear."
> Ancient saying: "We are given two ears and one mouth."
> Paul Tillich: "The first duty of love is to listen."

Talking

Talking is not just preparing remarks and letting fly. We improve if we carefully assess how opponents seem to be taking in what we have to say. For example, our team of U.S. conflict resolution specialists were to meet for a full week with a group of Cuban diplomats, Foreign Ministry and international affairs professionals, professors of diplomacy, and a few senior diplomacy students. On our first teaching day in Havana, in April 1995, Bill Lincoln's early comments had to do with taking stock of what is happening when we speak:

The first ingredient in the negotiations definition is to deal with proper communication. Is it noise? Are people really hearing what we're saying, in terms of fact, and in terms of the emotional context about it? Are we really sending a message that is full, that is complete, that is comprehensive, not only in fact, but tells truly where we're coming from in terms of our spirit, our hopes, our fears? (1995, p. 19)

Jourard (1978) was concerned about similar questions:

What is dialogue, in that it so seldom happens? It is, first of all, catching someone's attention so he or she listens to what you are saying. And it is your dialogue partner giving you evidence that he or she hears and understands, or at least wants to do so. This implies a capacity to imagine, or tune in to the reality of what is being said, the phenomenological reality of the speaker's world. Then dialogue calls for the listener to speak truth in relevant response. The goal is to understand and make oneself understood, so each participant shares in the world of the other's truth. This sharing is an offering and an opening, not the imposing of oneself or the self-negating "swallowing" of another person's views. (p. 49)

Fisher, Kopelman, and Schneider (1994) remind us that "before attempting to communicate our own view of a problem to someone with whom we are in disagreement, it is often wise to go through his concerns and arguments first, and to convey our comprehension of them." (p. 29) Also, see Rogers and Roethlisberger (1952) as they explore dialogue methods by means of which to understand the other with more clarity and compassion.

Understanding

All of the preparation, the listening, the talking prepares us to negotiate in the most fertile ways. What we learn can enable us to broaden our capacities to serve. In Jourard's words, "education is enlargement of the capacity for dialogue and the enlargement of awareness." (p. 48)

"Understanding," Fisher, Kopelman, and Schneider (1994) reminds us, "is not simply an intellectual activity. Feeling empathetically how others may feel can be as important as thinking clearly about what others may think." (p. 33)

Thinking of important negotiations they have ahead, a Cuban diplomatic leader, Dr. Oscar Garcia, (Cuba, 1995) put it this way: "(We must) plan to talk about what is in our hearts and on our minds." (p. 14)

Fisher, Kopelman, and Schneider (1994) write:

If we want to affect what is going on in the heads of others, we will want to be aware of emotions and motivations that may be surging through their hearts...Especially when we are communicating by letter, cable, fax, or telephone, we may be so concerned with ourselves or with substantive ideas that we ignore feelings on their part – feelings that are likely to drown out rational arguments. (p. 24)

Existence between the Poles of the Paradox

In an extraordinary set of four entwined novels by Lawrence Durrell, the Alexandria Quartet (1961), one reads the fine first novel, complete in itself and told from the point of view of one of the four main characters, and one comes away with a clear sense of what happened and why. When one begins the second novel in this quartet, an eerie feeling begins to rise because, told from the point of view of a second of the four main characters, one begins to see that what one thought happened, and why, begins to alter fundamentally. Things weren't as one thought. New, different perspectives emerge. At the end of the second novel, one is convinced that one has a true picture now with the two characters' points of view combined. But then begins the third novel, told from the third main character's perspective, and all sense of reality begins to float back into the air, because the third character sees the same set of events very differently indeed. The same happens with the fourth. Each novel is a distinct and separate reality, each one quite true, at least from the perspective of that one key person. In the great movie, <u>Roshomon</u>, four characters who each seemingly witnessed a murder give entirely contradictory accounts of the reality of what happened. Why do I cite these two works of art?

Our consulting firm would often first see labor and management leaders of public jurisdictions when the sides were preparing for a major strike, or in the midst of one, and wanted a neutral party to help them talk together with their opponents before the conflict got even worse. Typically, their views would be polarized, each group feeling that its side held the only legitimate position and that the other side was wrong, a side populated by fools or worse.

In our work, we would coach the parties to listen to the other side again and, deeper, again. We would begin to discover together that there was invariably an important element of truth in each side's position. This recognition would initially produce shock and disorientation. If in the world there is always only one true reality, and if the warring parties each believe an opposite reality, how can both, opposite sides hold truth? A fine paradox emerges. What do you do when opposites are true? If they are also right, what do we do now?

Scott Peck (1987) tells us that "the capacity to accept ambiguity and to think paradoxically is...one...of the requirements of peace-making." (p. 220)

In all the preceding discussion of ways to develop collaborative interest-based negotiation, this chapter has repeatedly focused on the need to get in touch with the other side, to hear the other side, empathize with them, grow to understand them, have compassion with them, and begin to think creatively about how to incorporate the other side's interests in the proposals for settlement you want to develop. Jourard understood that the needs for developing transparency were broad indeed. In negotiation, as the parties learn to communicate their perspectives and needs, and study those of the other side with more open eyes, it is more likely that polarization can begin to fall away....and their dialogue will deepen.

Tomson reminds us that individual distortions of reality are most likely to occur whenever we assume an "either/or" perspective." (p. 45) And further, "in Taoism, it is believed that when one is unaware that the two sides of a duality support one another to form the whole, he/she identifies with only one side of the polarity." (p. 25)

In the face of conflict and confusion about what to believe, Jourard (1978) tells us, "if he or she cannot speak, if I do not listen, or if I cannot understand, then we must remain suspicious strangers to one another, uncognizant of our authentic similarities and differences...."

But then Jourard goes to the possibility that there, too, is the turning point: "...when another speaks to me in truth, he or she becomes a transparent self and releases in me an imaginative experience of his or her existence." (p. 49)

This is the juncture where one can properly say the relationship unfolding begins to develop the character Martin Buber described as "I-Thou."   In an I-Thou relationship, one communicates with the other in all respect, as one would wish oneself to be treated, as one would treat a beloved.

In the shamanistic view of well-being, one evolves from a state of psychic and physical dis-integration into "the still point between the pairs of opposites" (Halifax, 1979, p. 20) from which point of view one can appreciate the truth and reality of each of the conflicting points of view." Here too one can sincerely honor those who hold the other view, seeing that the other view too has a valid reality and valid interests which can be integrated into a creative final proposal.

Ironically, in the large scheme of things, even if one were to remain at a selfish, self-centered level, exclusively concerned for the welfare of one's own self and one's own team, one still would find that the best way to protect one's team is to find an equitable and lasting settlement of the dispute at hand. For the settlement to be lasting, it must be reasonably equitable. For it to be equitable, it must incorporate the opposite team's primary needs.

Drawing a partial analogy from another distance, Tomson (1996) reminds us that "Jung observed that the way his clients resolved important problems was not by solving the problems logically, but rather by achieving 'a new level of consciousness' from which the problems 'faded out'." (p. 41)

I don't generally expect concrete differences and problems in negotiation to completely "fade out." Yet I have seen time and time again the initial urgent feelings of polarization fall away and be partly or fully replaced by a sense of common ground, working together. Fisher, Kopelman and Schneider (1994) put it this way:

> Conflict is inevitable. It will not disappear, nor can it be ignored. For better or for worse, we will have to cope with conflicting interests as long as we live...Fortunately, conflict is not all bad. Differences can be a source of value. The fact that we have different priorities may mean that each of us can attain something important to us without injury to anything important to someone else...Doing better is not a matter of producing good answers out of thin air, but a matter of asking a series of questions which are likely to result in coping more skillfully with an endless flow of conflicting interests....Every tool is intended to ask questions or to stimulate better questions. (p. 176)

Labor and management negotiating teams working with our consulting group rather consistently discovered in time (and with the right continuation of personnel leaders who were learning to trust each other) how to act almost as a <u>single</u> focused working group, as a developing team in their joint committee we would facilitate, to explore and research the means by which to find common solutions to problems in common. Initially called in to handle crises, our consulting group was often asked (after the hostilities were resolved which initially brought us into the case) to stay and facilitate ongoing monthly collaborative labor-management meetings for what have sometimes turned out to be years of team-intensive collaborative planning thereafter. As Bill Lincoln has pointed out, the parties (as former opponents) can discover in each other the partners they have needed all along.

The late Louise Diamond (1996) (of the Institute for Multi-Track Diplomacy, in Washington, D.C., which she and retired U.S. Ambassador John McDonald started and operated) describes how she saw the potential for transforming negotiation. She defined transformed negotiation as:

> ...different from managing or resolving conflict. To transform conflict is to work systematically to change the very assumptions, beliefs, and perceptions of the parties in conflict, as well as to open the doors to creative solutions and new behaviors...to release the energy bound in...patterns over time, and to reshape that energy into new and more positive patterns of relationship.... (p. 2)

Whether working through a particular conflict or seeking to further transform conflicts within that organization or social system, there is the basic need to come together to work problems through with dignity, empathy, and understanding. Ambassador John McDonald focuses such a change in a description he gave during the 1995 CRI-ISRI-IMTD Cuba exchange in which we both taught:

> ...In the first instance, we had opposing views. And...we managed to shift (from) having opposing viewpoints to having a common viewing point. So...we began to look at the problem together, collectively and collaboratively, solving the problem. We owned the problem together, and I think that was a major shift. (Tape 18A, p. 1)

Conclusion

We have arrived: It is the 21st century. We find escalating crises and strife on nearly every side. Our world grows smaller daily as cultures bump into each other with little understanding but with greater and greater power. Public expenditures drop while compelling basic human need across the world escalates drastically. The disparity between haves and have-nots deepens into a chasm ever more vast. Almost all new income goes to the already rich. The earth itself hangs in the balance. All the difficulties we have to face remind us that more humane and potent methods of negotiation are profoundly needed and, hopefully, can develop.

Especially in the midst of these high-stakes challenges, Sidney Jourard was prescient in his sense of the crucial role of honest sharing and joint exploration. Jourard's quest for transparency fits the quest for collaborative interest-based (basic human needs-based) negotiation like a key in a lock.

On the last afternoon of our Cuban exchange, one Cuban participant looked out the window and wondered aloud:

Wouldn't it be wonderful if conflict resolution became another language of the world? If everybody had the same language, and–before they resorted to force and violence and treachery to resolve disputes–(they) would say, wait, there's another way to do this; let's sit down. Let's see if we can negotiate this and have your interests and my interests somehow be satisfied. (Cuban transcript)

These thinker/practitioners have not only begun the development of linked fields with ramifications across many disciplines. They challenge us to see our way through the crises before us. They challenge us to envision our ways toward a more humane sustainable social commons developed through more humane social processes and that through these more humane approaches to conflict and its resolution, we may glimpse vistas of peace and sustainability which may lie beyond – which must lie beyond.

Fisher, Kopelman, and Schneider (1994, p. 67) in <u>Beyond Machiavelli</u> tell of a story from Italian folklore. Three workers are cutting stones in the hot sun. When the first is asked what he is doing, he replies, "I am chipping these stones to make them just the right size." The second replies, "I am earning my wages." To the same question, the third replies: "I am building a cathedral."

⚬⚭⚬

Acknowledgements

The author has explored a number of the ideas in these chapters over recent years in his discussions with William Lincoln, Executive Director of the Lincoln Institue, CRI (the Conflict Resolution, Research, and Resource Institute, Inc.,) and President of NCA (National Center Associates, Inc.), of Tacoma, Washington. Several of the ideas have taken further shape in the author's dialogues with the late Arthur Warmoth, Ph.D., Professor of Psychology, Sonoma State University; retired U.S. Ambassador John McDonald, Chairman, IMTD (Institute for Multi-Track Diplomacy, Inc.), Washington, D.C.; Tom Greening, Ph.D., Professor of Psychology, Saybrook Graduate School, and (the University of California, Los Angeles, UCLA;, Jon Townsend, M.A., Principal, Agreements Work, Inc., West Linn, Oregon, and Jan Cimonin, artist extraordinaire,

The unpublished writings of Douglas Tomson, M.A., regarding Jourard's perspectives on personal transparency and the research and philosophical milieu around the concept, have proved invaluable, most especially Tomson's review of particular perceptual distortions, ones which can be seen among adversaries. (This author considers Tomson co-author of much of that four-page section in this chapter, but Tomson demurs and says the footnoting shows his contribution.)

Adele Amodeo, M.P.H., provided critical and systematic text editing. Cesca Flynn was a most valuable editorial assistant.

The author first presented some of the key material in this chapter in April 1995 in Havana, Cuba, at the Instituto Superior de Relaciones Internacionales (ISRI), the Senior Diplomatic Graduate School within Cuba's Foreign Ministry, as part of the cultural and educational exchange and research project held between ISRI and CRI, and co-sponsored by IMTD.

The ISRI-CRI-IMTD spring 1995 venture became categorized by the U.S. Department of the Treasury as an official research project.

From final questionnaires filled out by all the Cuban participants at the end of the week of intense seminar, this Cuba project drew **98%** favorable ratings for the excellence of the learning and **99%** favorable ratings for pertinence to individual Cuban seminar participants' lives.

References

Anonymous. (1958). A New Theory of Schizophrenia. <u>Journal of Abnormal and Social Psychology, 57</u>.

Bloch, A. (1980). <u>The Complete Murphy's Law.</u> Los Angeles: Price Stern Sloan, Inc.

Bloch, A. (1990). <u>Murphy's law - Book Two.</u> Los Angeles: Price Stern Sloan, Inc.

Buber, M. (1958). <u>I and Thou.</u> New York: Scribner.

Cameron, N. & Margaret, A. (1951). <u>Behavior Pathology.</u> Boston: Houghton Mifflin.

Cozer, L. (1964). <u>The Functions of Social Conflict.</u> New York: Free Press.

Cuba (1995, April). Unpublished 300 page text of cultural and educational exchange and research project, sponsored by CRI-ISRI, co-sponsored by IMTD (Conflict Resolution, Research, and Resource Institute, Instituto Superior de Relaciones Internacionales, and Institute for Multi-Track Diplomacy),

April 5-9, 1995, Havana, Cuba. Chapter 3 in my <u>On the Midnight Train: Moscow to Leningrad</u>.

Darwin, C. (1937). <u>Origin of Species.</u> Harvard Classics Vol. 11. New York: Collier:

Diamond, L. (1996). <u>Beyond Win/Win: The Heroic Journey of Conflict Transformation</u>. Washington, D.C.: Institute for Multi-Track Diplomacy.

Durrell, L. (1961). <u>Alexandria Quartet</u>. New York: Dutton.

Fisher, R., Kopelman, E. & Schneider, A. K. (1994). <u>Beyond Machiavelli–Tools For Coping with Conflict</u>. Cambridge: Harvard University Press.

Fisher, R. & Ury, W. (1981). <u>Getting to Yes</u>. New York: Penguin.

Fisher, W.F. (1985). Self-Deception: An Empirical-Phenomenological Inquiry into its Essential Meanings. In A. Giorgi, (Ed.), <u>Phenomenology and Psychological Research</u>. Pittsburgh: Duquesne University Press.

Halifax, J. (1979). <u>Shamanic Voices</u>. New York: E. P. Dutton.

Horney, K. (1958). <u>Neurosis and Human Growth</u>. New York: W.W. Norton.

Johnsen, B. (1966). Private e-mail letter. September 7.

Jourard, S. (1978, Winter). Education as Dialogue. <u>Journal of Humanistic Psychology</u>. 18(1).

Jourard, S. (1994). In Lowman, M., Jourard, A. & Jourard, M. Editors. Selected writings. Marina del Rey: Round Right Press.

Jourard, S. (1964). The Transparent Self. Princeton: Van Nostrand.

Kaiser, H. (1965). Effective Psychotherapy. New York: Free Press.

Keen, S. (1986). Faces of the Enemy: Reflections of a Hostile Imagination. San Francisco: Harper & Row.

Lincoln, W. F. (1995). In Pursuit of Promises: The practitioner's course in collaborative negotiations and cooperative problem solving–A practical experience in transformed negotiations. Preliminary draft.

Lincoln, W. F. (1990). Comments during classroom teaching, Oakland CA.

Lincoln, W. F. (1995). Comments during classroom teaching, Instituto Superior de Relaciones Internacionales, Havana, Cuba.

Lincoln, W. F. In Townsend, J. & Robinson, S. (Ed.) (1998). Mediation. Psychology of mediation class reader, Sonoma State University, p. 10.

Maslow, A. (1968). Toward a Psychology of Being. New York: Van Nostrand Reinhold.

McDonald, J. (1995). Unpublished Cuba exchange interview transcript, Tape 18A, p. 1.

McWilliams, C. (1962). The Responsibility of the Student Community to Society. In S. Robinson, (Editor). Readings in Student Community Involvement. Philadelphia: U. S. National Student Association.

Peck, M. S. (1987). Different Drum. New York: Simon and Schuster.

Pennebaker, J.W. (1993). Putting Stress into Words: Health, Linguistics, and Therapeutic Implications. Behavioral Research and Therapy. 31(6).

Pennebaker, J.W. & Beall, S. (1986). Confronting a Traumatic Event: Toward an Understanding of Inhibition and Disease. Journal of Abnormal Psychology. 95.

Pennebaker, J.W., Hughes, C. & O'Heeron, Roc. (1987). The Psychophysiology of Confession: Linking Inhibitory and Psychosomatic Processes. Journal of Personality and Social Psychology. 52.

Rogers, C. & Roethlisberger, F.J. (1952). "Barriers and Gateways to Communication," Harvard Business Review, Vol. XXX, #4, July-August 1952, pp. 46-52.

Schaller, L.E. (1966). Community Organization: Conflict and Reconciliation. New York: Abingdon Press.

Sun Tzu. (1988). The Art of War. Boston: Shambhala.

CHAPTER 4

Coming Back From Polarization: Listening and Transparency in Psychotherapy and Mediation

Applications of Jourard, Lincoln, Fischer, Ury, Maslow, Keen, Kopelman, Rogers, and Schneider

(Please note that this chapter was originally drafted to be part of a mediation publication to be translated and published in Russian in Russia, to interpret current thoughts briefly to a new audience.)

Table of Contents

Quick summary

Much of bargaining in recent times has been characterized by increasing polarization, which is common in adversarial bargaining. Cooperative interest-based bargaining about basic and fundamental human needs and interests is a good and increasingly used alternative to the adversarial. Transparent talking and actively listening in tandem can significantly increase progress toward fair and enduring resolutions. Final thoughts on growing steps include notes on paradox, multiple legitimate realities, and the effect of sharing tales of suffering.

Polarization and transparency

It is understandable that people accustomed to adversarial negotiations, ones unfamiliar with collaborative interest-based negotiations (or without trust in it), would be skeptical of this approach. Sidney Jourard, the late American psychologist, theorist and teacher, wanted people and organizations involved in psychotherapeutic healing, problem-solving, and peace-making to explore increasing the practice of transparency. Without it, as he saw it, dysfunctional dynamics tend to grow, interlace, become more complex to unravel, threatening resolution. Not listening, anger, distortion, and a number of problems from adversarial negotiation may lead into questionable communications and more polarization. (Note: For a study of negative psychological effects of adversarial negotiation, such as perception distortion, see Chapter 3: "Transparency and Interest-Based Collaborative Negotiation About Basic Human Needs," which goes into greater detail on the number of negative effects shown and developed there and noted more briefly in this chapter.)

Fisher and Ury explain that "we often handle conflict poorly because we are each prisoners of our own thinking….We tend to collect evidence that supports our prior views and to dismiss or ignore nonconforming data. The more we become convinced of our views, the more we filter out information that would lead us to question them." (pp. 21-22) In the beginning of Out of Egypt, the protagonist says that the more he feels his anger rising, the more he is convinced that he is right. (The reptilian part of our brain emerging here works quite differently from the problem-solving prefrontal cortex.)

Cooperative interest-based bargaining about basic and fundamental human needs and interests

In The Transparent Self, Sidney Jourard (1964) differentiates collaborative interest-based negotiation from adversarial negotiation, as follows. Whereas adversarial negotiation seeks to be opaque for self-protection and keeping the other party blind, cooperative interest-based negotiation seeks through humanistic and transpersonal ways to have the parties work more transparently together to find mutually fulfilling solutions.

Bill Lincoln (1990) states the caution that if an "opponent's" proposal doesn't meet the client's key interests, interests which can be clearly identified and listed, the adversary's proposal can be dismissed on the spot and actions can be taken accordingly."

Such books as the best-seller, Getting to Yes (Fisher & Ury, 1981) and In Pursuit of Promises (Lincoln, 1995), show how the approach of collaborative interest-based bargaining has so much to offer the person frustrated with adversarial bargaining, with the old and battered standard.

These persons often want to explore more collaborative interest-based work and cooperatively search for common ground.

Using a collaborative interest-based method looking at basic human needs and interests often stimulates much deeper and better conversation and hearing that can lead toward each party ending up walking away from the negotiation table as a substantial "winner," along with the others.

It should come as no surprise that principles in cooperative interest-based conflict resolution, especially mediation, regularly parallel processes in psychotherapeutic healing.

One can follow Abraham Maslow's hierarchy of human needs, going up the needs ladder step by step, from the most primitive needs (such as safe air, safe food, water, and shelter) up through self-actualization and, empathetically, up to the high needs of our common nature, toward transpersonal actualization.

In Lincoln's view, "specific basic human needs and interests contain crucial principles, values, belief systems, those which "need" to be satisfied if the conflict before the parties is to be equitably, practically, legally, and durably resolved".

As one becomes more conscious of the dynamics and substance of the negotiations of which one is a part, one can increasingly look for those interests and issues which one and one's opponent have in common.

Seeking out the other party's interests and needs in negotiation and mediation leads to increased clarity. It is considered imperative for the parties in therapy to gain such understanding. Fisher and Ury (1981) advocate reversing roles in one's mind to try to empathize with how the other side is thinking and feeling. How does the other person feel? How does the child understand the situation's tension? What is the other's reality? "Role reversal and the other techniques discussed above not only help us understand another's point of view, they help us find room to maneuver by illuminating needs and concerns that lie below the surface."(p. 46) Lincoln adds that "effective negotiators often prepare a chart that compares the elements of their proposals with the other side's interests, and then try to test the other side's receptivity to proposals before they are even offered. Areas of overlap will serve as areas for possible compromise...." (p. 202) Therapists often urge their clients to do this with those from whom they are becoming estranged.

Interest-based dialogue opens up psychotherapy and negotiations. Whether negotiations are occurring in the family, the workplace, or internationally, negotiators (sometimes through mediation) seek clear language to have clearer communications with the other side(s). Lincoln encourages negotiators to "learn why an offer is being made or resisted...for such will always be related to interest satisfaction or interest dissatisfaction." Increasing transparency enables the parties to learn more about each other's priorities and thus prepares them to figure out how to incorporate the other side and their side's primary needs into cooperatively fashioned solutions.

Such solutions have a better chance of being accepted with the resultant agreement having a significantly better chance of becoming durable. (p. 208)

"No durable settlement agreement is possible unless significant self-interests for all disputants are satisfied at acceptable levels – all things considered." (Lincoln, 1995, p. 210)

Transparent talking combined with active, empathetic listening

Transparent talk is the opposite of a poker-like approach. No "dead-pan" impenetrability. Nor is talking just coming up with remarks and letting them loose. And Fisher, Kopelman, and Schneider (1994) state that "before attempting to communicate our own view of a problem to someone with whom we are in disagreement, it is often wise to go through his concerns and arguments first and to convey our comprehension of them." (p. 29)

Also, see Rogers and Roethlisberger (1952) as they explore powerful dialogue methods by means of which to hear and understand the other with significantly more clarity and compassion.

Roger Fisher and William Ury (1981) observe that "angry people often fail to hear what others have to say. And whatever they hear, they are likely to put the worst possible interpretation on both the words and actions of someone who is seen as an adversary." (p. 24)

Vivekananda talked about our brain's "drunken monkeys". In our minds, we can honestly be trying to listen to someone but our "drunken monkeys" are jumping, swinging, and hooting, leaving little room for real, full listening. We need to calm down. They can too.

Half a century ago, Carl Rogers, the late psychological theorist and practitioner, mapped out a method to develop active listening. Quieting down inside, breathing deeply, focusing on the other person and what that person is trying to say, allowing for emotional room, for empathy, for compassion, for considering the other's being. (<u>Harvard Business Review</u>, Summer 1952) Sixty years later, it still may be the best writing on the subject.

Jourard (1978) could sense how crucial the listening process could be to developing trust and transparency. To understand the other, we must listen. Jourard said, "while education is not only listening, listening is a necessary part of it....It is no small thing really to listen....What we hear said to us can be a matter of life and death." (p. 50)

Listening and what we can discover by listening can make all the difference, especially in situations of great importance. It is widely felt among professional conflict resolution people that active listening, empathetic listening is the single most important skill to develop; so much emerges from there.

"The first requirement of love is to listen."

Across paradox – multiple valid realities

F. Scott Fitzgerald: "The sign of a first-rate mind is the ability to hold two contradictory positions and not lose the ability to function." The mediator and therapist both need to develop this basic skill for their practices. Scott Peck (1987) adds that "the capacity to accept ambiguity and to think paradoxically is...one...of the requirements of peacemaking." (p. 220)

Paradox is a condition where apparently irreconcilable opposites both appear to be true. Yet when we study such a situation, we find that *each* side holds important elements of the truth.

Fortunately, the paradox actually can be the doorway at the start of the next stage of deliberation together. I wondered then:

What if each side were encouraged to listen again to the other side? What if each side realized that the other side had legitimate needs and interests to satisfy as well? How could both sides win. How could the "opposites" find a creative way to blend a solution? To find reasonable satisfaction for BOTH sides? ALL sides.

So, let's take a mediation-facilitation-system redesign case in which both sides had legitimacy: a labor-management crisis on the verge of a strike in an East Bay city for which labor and management asked us to help. After finding in initial caucuses what seemed like remarkable truth on <u>both</u> sides, when we gathered the sides together for our first joint session, we asked each side to listen again and more attentively to the other side's worries, suffering, and alternative ideas for resolution.

When parties did so, listened well, spoke clearly about their needs, the sides seemed to realize the other side had legitimacy in what they wanted – it ceased being two antagonistic teams: It began what seemed more like "a single team with a serious problem in common to solve".

Brainstorming solutions – Exploring alternatives

In the case just mentioned, an East Bay city, when each side reached the point of realizing the deep legitimacy of the other side's point of view, labor and management came together to collaborate in a session in which everyone was encouraged to make proposals to advance an idea they had on how to solve problems. They soon came up with 14 proposals on heavy paper, which they put up all around the walls of the council chamber. (Note that different forms of psychotherapy, as well as the Organization Development field, use problem-solving methods like this.) By asking them to begin to choose, we helped them work the preferred proposals back down to two top favorite solutions - and then reached a complicated but equitable and durable solution which entertwined the two. All parties agreed, their constituencies agreed, and we were done for the present. (Labor and management leadership subsequently asked that we come monthly to meet with them for a labor-management cooperative session on anticipating and doing studies of upcoming problems together. This meeting arrangement continued for about three years.)

Humanistic and transpersonal psychology

The humanistic psychology movement grew in influence in the 60's and 70's and developed theory, clinical practice, and the national and international human potential movement. This in turn influenced the furthering of humanistic values in both psychotherapy and in the development of modern theory and practice in such fields as organization development and the development of cooperative interest-based, democratic conflict resolution. (Note that this thinking is grounded in Abraham Maslow's Hierarchy of Human Needs.)

Toward the end of his life, Maslow, one of the parents of the humanistic psychology movement and the human potential movement, refocused his efforts almost totally toward the coming into being of a coalition calling itself transpersonal psychology, how humans are intimately and inextricably connected – As the Free Dictionary says: "bound together by an inextricable fate". (Meanwhile, combined computer/brain studies are discovering more powerful brain-to-brain connections, which underscore the theory.

In this last stage of his life, Maslow posited an even stronger connection among people touched on in his previous "self-actualization " concept, at the old apex of his hierarchy of human needs. According to colleagues, he decided in his mind on a firm new "transpersonal actualization" top to his hierarchy of needs. He, Tony Sutich and others formed an association, started publications. But relatively soon, Maslow was dead. Still, the movement continued to grow in the U.S. and has become an important internationally growing force of thought. In the transpersonal way, one develops more empathy and even can grow into identity with the other party. What might be the potential effect of this empathy growing toward compassion in the resolution of conflict?

Sharing tales of suffering

> "Allah husamahus salaam"
> "The name of God is love"

The Zen master Thich Nhat Hanh says mediation can even succeed using only one approach: The mediator goes to one side and learns all about the suffering of that side. The mediator goes to the other side and deeply learns their suffering as well. Then the mediator goes to each side and helps them listen to the suffering of the other side. According to him, then the healing will begin.

His Holiness the Dalai Lama says that the better we know people, the closer to impossible it is for us to sit by and watch them suffer. This would help explain why when disputants reach a stage of becoming strongly empathetic or even compassionate about the needs of the other side, as well as their own, a more cooperative creative approach to resolution can emerge and flow with more momentum toward innovative solutions. Think of it as positive lightning.

At this turn, the parties can find their logical and defensive and offensive primitive thought getting more settled and balanced by empathy and compassion.

Another way of shedding light on this advanced stage of development, Dr. Martin Buber speaks of a deeply needed movement from I-it relationships (treating the other more or less as a thing) to I-Thou relationships (treating others as family, as loved ones, and as another side of oneself). "Understanding," Fisher, Kopelman, and Schneider (1994) remind us, "is not simply an intellectual activity. Feeling empathetically how others may feel can be as important as thinking clearly about what others may think." (p. 33). They write: If we want to affect what is going on in the heads of others, we will want to be aware of emotions and motivations that may be surging through their hearts. (p. 24)

In considering the important discussions they had ahead, a Cuban leader, Dr. Oscar Garcia, (Cuba, 1995), former Cuban Ambassador to Spain, then Rector of the Instituto Superior de Relaciones Internacionales, (ISRI) said that, after all these years: "(We must) plan to talk about what is in our hearts and on our minds." (p. 14)).

Effect of a new level of consciousness
Here to end this chapter is a intriguing thought: Tomson (1996) notes that "Jung observed that the way his clients resolved important problems was not [necessarily] by solving the problems logically, but rather by achieving 'a new level of consciousness' from which the problems 'faded out'." (p. 41)

Acknowledgements

This paper could not have been written without collaborative dialogue over the years, especially with NCA/CRI Executive Director and Lincoln Institute President Bill Lincoln; fellow teachers Jon Townsend, Agreements Work, Inc.; Dr. Art Warmoth, Professor Emeritus, Sonoma State University; Bruce Johnsen, Monterey; and retired U.S. Ambassador John McDonald, head of the Institute for Multi-Track Diplomacy.

Brief Bibliography

Buber, M. (1970) I and Thou (W. Kaufman translator) New York: Charles Scribner's Sons

Fischer, R., Kopelman, E., and Schneider, A.K. (1994) Beyond Machiavelli: Tools for Coping with Conflict Cambridge MA: Harvard University Press

Fisher, R. and Ury, W. (1981). Getting to Yes. New York: Houghton-Mifflin

Jourard, S.M. (1978). Education as Dialogue, Journal of Humanistic Psychology, 18 (1), 47-52

Jourard, S.M. (1964) The Transparent Self. New York: Van Nostrand Reinhold

Keen, S. (1988) Faces of the Enemy. San Francisco: Harper Collins

Lincoln, W.L. (1990) Training, Oakland CA.

Lincoln, W.L. (1995) In Pursuit of Promises: The Practitioner's Course in Collaborative Negotiations and Cooperative

Problem-Solving Tacoma: Conflict Resolution, Research & Resource Institute, Inc.

Peck, M.S. ((1987) The Different Drum. Community-Making and Peace New York: Simon and Schuster

Robinson, R.P. (Skip) (1999). Transparency and Interest-Based Collaborative Negotiation About Basic Human Needs, chapter in Invitations to Dialogue: The Legacy of Sidney M. Jourard, Kendall/Hunt Publishing Company

Robinson, R.P. (Skip), Wallach, J., and Amodeo, A. (1990; 2003) Paradox and its Resolution in the Health Plan Benefits Crisis, Northern California Council on Mediation; Association for Humanistic Psychology Perspective

Rogers, C. and Roethlisberger, F.J. (1952), Barriers and Gateways to Communication, Harvard Business Review XXX (4), 46-52.

Tomson, D. (1997) Self-Disclosure and Healthy Personality: A Historical and Conceptual Analysis, Masters Abstract International 35(4), 1067 UMI Order # AA1383971

Charles Webel (Spring 1996) The Human Sciences and the Human Prospect," Saybrook Perspective.

CHAPTER 5

Helping Others Come Back From Polarization

What if you find yourself working with one or more bargaining parties who have apparently regressed? Perhaps they have regressed to the limbic system/reptilian brain level at which the person's thoughts and actions are operating at a much more primitive level. (One could expect significantly elevated cortisol levels and more in the blood of the parties in conflict. One could expect more anger, more wildness, perhaps disdain, perhaps aggression, and very little accurate listening.) What if you know you want to work on bringing the party or parties back to refocus on the work of resolving the conflict? What if you also want to reestablish positive and functional relationships. Tough job. But think about using some of the steps below:

> (Note: Of course to start with, if you come to be in this situation, you can alter the meeting by having the parties take a good long break for breathing and for calming down, by re-scheduling the meeting, by scheduling a separate caucus for each party to the conflict, by scheduling one-to-one meetings, by going home to start again another day.)

STARTING POINT of the process: One can re-energize the process, ironically, through one's own stillness-quietness—centering—slowing down - paying attention to breathing – sitting up straight posture – feet solidly on the ground. Such stillness abets grounding and re-centering, which can be a silent model for others to consider, which is the starting point. One can even do this quietly right in a group setting. One can also take a step further and ask the other or others if they would like to try doing this together. (Note the work on this of Dr. Carl Rogers and HH the Dalai Lama.) (Note: Interestingly enough, such activities can also significantly drop the cortisol level in the blood.)

The parties will need to begin to consider developing an agree-ment or agreements on the procedures both sides can agree to for meeting together. By doing so, chances can increase that the talks will be safer and more productive for the participants. This in turn can help release creativity to work toward resolution.

It will be important to keep considering three key sat-isfactions which all parties will need during and after the dialogue: • procedural satisfaction (a sense that the meeting's collaboratively developed procedures are work-ing fairly), • psychological satisfaction (sense and intuition that things are getting back on target), and • substantive satisfaction (a sense that overall the concrete terms of the contract developing are going to be satisfactory). Fortunately, parties can put their own active curiosity to work on finding a better "fit".

Employ "active listening" with the other party. Each party spends time in active listening with the other side and spends time talking with increasing transparently, honestly, deeply to the other side. Understanding and empathy can now grow better. Factual and motivational issues can become clearer with the improved listen-ing. (Note the work of Dr. Carl Rogers).

"Transparent" talk by one side balances with the active listening and centering by the other side. (Note again the work of Dr. Sidney Jourard.). These activities so far can facilitate a more accurate mutual one-to-one communication process, so important as the parties work toward resolution.

In recent brain science, it is being found that a process called "looping" begins, neural and biochemical processes in each party, the "formation between two brains of a functional link, a feedback loop that crosses the skin-and-skull barrier between bodies". Perceptions and judgments can begin to change. (In research, this effect is so powerful and integrating between them, that parties are increasingly said to "co-create each other".) (See the work on social intelligence of Dr. Daniel Goleman.)

(During the steps below, movement can increase perceptually and biochemically from I-it toward I-Thou.

At a step deeper, and in turn, each party expresses more of what deep suffering is going on among those of its own side, because of this conflict. This is done in earnest with and to each other, perhaps with facilitation, while the other side is actively listening. Both sides get heard out much deeper. Active, empathetic listening makes these descriptions of the other side's suffering of much more impact.

The parties can begin to bridge a conflict paradox – Each side begins to understand the other side (and its different reality) more and, with this, experience growing empathy and compassion. One can see and feel an easing off of the polarization and the stereotyping.

The parties can make strides toward recognizing that each party may have a separate reality it understands and is following. This may make a case of multiple valid realities. (Rather than each side feeling they have the "only" truth.) (Both sides have elements of truth and good sense in their own positions. One studies how to creatively meld each party's high priority needs toward a collaborative resolution which optimizes both sides' needs satisfaction, shared success.) (Each party can better reassess the nature, character, and fairness of what the other party's reality is seeking.) (With a little more trust, which can build in this kind of safer atmosphere, transparent talk and active listening each way can increase and intensify.)

The parties can begin to reframe the matters to be negotiated into basic human needs and also into needs they believe they may have in common. (There may also be elements that are complementary or different.) (This can be a change from priority "positions" in negotiation toward satisfaction of priority "interests" each is trying to solve for.) (Even opposed interests can ease as more can be worked on in common.)

Opponents begin to appear more like "the partners we have been seeking". (Note the work of Bill Lincoln.)

Beyond self-actualization, transpersonal actualization begins and increases. In transparent actualization, the person realizes that he/she actually joins in and becomes aware of a literal kind of union with the other party.

Parties increasingly cooperate in collaborative research they need to follow together and integrative proposal development they become able to do.

(When the steps above have taken place, a problem may literally "dissolve". Note Dr. Carl Jung's observation that this dissolving happened regularly in his psychiatric practice.) At least, by this point, the parties will certainly be more amenable to working things out – and probably have more ideas about how to resolve the conflict and how to make the resolution last.

The parties creatively find ways to agree on a settlement they have been developing together using their growing collaborative skills, which they have tested and which they believe will prove to be durable and sustainable.   Productive dialogue channels open again and begin again to flow.

White, white

1. The woods in the Marin hills

The dancers turn and turn
in a circle, the party guests
at Sat Santokh's 50th birthday.
(I join in and remember with a sigh,
I will be fifty in a few weeks.)
In the white and yellow light,
sweat shows on the dancers' foreheads.
The Sufi song ends. Shams takes a breath,
has been beating the drum,
announces a new dance.

In white turban, long beard,
white clothes, Sat Santokh beams.
"This next is one of my favorites,"
he says. "One night, years ago,
when we were dancing this next dance,
I was doing the dance with my eyes closed.
While we danced, I experienced myself in a circle of
ancient elders. It was night. In the darkness,
we began dancing to the right
in a circle together around and
around a bonfire, bending down together
and raising up together, everyone
flickering in the light."

2. Juneau, Alaska

Falling all about me,
snowflakes the size of
pure white half-dollars,

white, white falling before my eyes,
riding up and down the icy wind,
mounds of white loading evergreen
tree branches, white trees in
thick stands in every direction
covering the surrounding mountains rising,
from the nearby edges of the small town,
rising almost straight up into the
freezing early evening air.

3. Oakland downtown, not far
from the Cypress Structure

I sit silently at my seventh floor desk
looking out over the city,
The end-of-the-day glancing sunlight
is almost white against the ornate
high wall of the 1906 building
across the street and almost
green against the fall hills in the distance.
The earthquake begins like any other.
Our administrative assistant Sarahjane and I
say to each other "oh, an earthquake",
as we turn to go on with our work.
This one begins to shake the building
harder ("this one is big," we say, turning back
to each other), then still harder, and way harder.
Our seventh-floor office has begun leaping up
and down, throttling us awake like children from
our beds, then, growing beyond bounds, a raging giant
thrashing back and forth as if frenzied to shake off
its clothes and come apart.

4. Leaving Juneau toward Anchorage

The silver and white airplane
hurdles us up into the morning air,
rising above the white-laden mountain
forest that disappears quickly
below banks of billowing white clouds.
Below the airplane, the clouds part
and snow-capped mountains one after
another after another appear. A white land,
punctuated by white-on-gray
jutting mountains, stretches
as far as I can see. A huge bay
of light blue and white water
reflecting the sky and clouds
floats by below, before the clouds
close their curtains again,
then open again. Dozens, then literally
hundreds of white-capped mountains appear
like vast unmoving herds of granite moose
and elk in counsel. A glacier pours
without motion from their midst,
its mile-wide ice flow held still
by the white-gloved hand of time.
"Not now," it whispers. "Not now."

Multi-veined waterways appear
criss-crossing the landscape below with
white ice and blue. A long river-width
waterway runs toward the horizon and
disappears among the mountain-after-
mountain-after-mountain track.

5.

The giant's frenzy thrashes our
fifteen-story brick building up and down,
back and forth, mad to get out of its cage
of brick and steel and blast in every direction.
Sarahjane and I dive for the floor in a doorway
by the hall and hold each other tight, on the floor,
covering each other's heads with our hands.

6.

My plane dips down toward Cordova.
Miles and miles of pure white,
mountain upon mountain – Out my window,
cloud curtain opens, shock, miles long, a huge
slap of absolute black against the white,
then another, like some immense
black paint river has washed over the lower
altitudes of these mountains-after-mountains:
everything else white, but for these
vast poison pools and rivers of black.

7.

Our windows explode as we hear
fifteen floors of glass crash out at once.
The mountain of glass flies down
toward the pavement below and hits
like a huge glass bomb. Stories of
stairway walls are breaking apart
and falling down the hall.

We captives are heaved wildly about.
The building can't possibly
shake any harder or must surely
collapse around us. Huddled
on the floor, we hold on to each other
as tight as we know how.

8.

A young woman from Cordova,
writing about what she sees
right after the oil spill:
"(Mom), the entire ecosystem
has died (here) or is dying.
The deer and bear (are gone)...

Ninety percent of the vast
natural area around me
is as silent as death."

9.

The wild thrashing continues
then begins to slow, then slows some more.
Then, for a few minutes, the floor vibrates
like a huge bell, then quivers and slowly quiets
to a halt. The room becomes very, very still.

10.

In a small wooden house
just up the snowy street

from the State Capitol, an Alaskan ecological
defense fund lawyer describes her work
coordinating law suits. She is very tired but precise,
animated. Her brown eyes are determined.

11.

Over lunch later, a young man and woman,
two leaders of Alaskan environmental organizations,
weave their study plans, their Greenprints, their vision
of pure ancient and future mountains, forests, animals, waters.

12.

While it is zero outside, the Chair
of the Alaska Oil Spill Commission sits
at a plain folding table on a folding chair
in his unadorned white conference room at the end
of our meeting and contemplates the outline
of his impending Report to the legislature,
weighs points in silence. We shake hands again
and begin putting on our heavy outer wraps.
We are agreed. I thank him for his unsung work.
I know of those outside Alaska who continue
counting on his Commission's impact for their safety
and for that of their future generations.
He smiles quietly, jokes about other things,
like what he'd have otherwise liked to do
with his Christmas, then says goodbye
and walks away slowly toward his office,
his back a little bent, his coat collar up on one side.
As he turns to go, his eyes appear to be somewhere else,
maybe up some white mountain pass way above the city,
in the utter white silence and freezing air.

13.

As early morning light slants across a makeshift room,
an already oily worker leans against the wall, stares across
the long room at the rows upon rows of open-mouthed
dead bodies of blackened animals, their eyes still open wide.
She bends over and begins to cry for souls.

14.

The pilot, panting, steers the fireboat
toward the raging Marina shoreline.
A fireman crawls inch by inch
under the crumbling house
to hold a terrified woman in his arms until
she is freed just before it crashes down with a roar.

15.

People climb the Cypress freeway structure like a mountain,
then quickly crawl under the broken concrete of the high
freeway, into the debris, even as the gas fumes begin to fill
the crushing space. They are calling out, calling out.

Human chains lift people up, carry other people
down. All around, people are standing in shock,
holding each other, searching for loved ones,
staring in disbelief at the ruins.

16.

It is late, time to go home.
I am so tired. So much has happened;
so much to do. I close Sat Santokh's

front door behind me. In the deep cool darkness
outside, a new friend and I walk down the long row
of fragrant wooden steps, the music coming from
inside, above and behind me. We walk carefully
down the steep longer driveway. Below, as I reach
the road in the blackness, I turn around
toward Sham's drumbeat one last time.
In the upper room, soft yellow light suffuses out
the windows into the night air, like glowing mist.

I can see the moving dancers near the windows,
still in a circle, their line bobbing, moving slowly
to the right together, bending down together,
singing "Yah," then rising up in unison,
all arms and hands reaching up, pointing up past
Sat Santokh's painted ceiling, singing "Allah!"
stepping together to the right again,
in unison bending down, singing "Yah",
the yellow mist of light almost white
against the dark green night trees,
all bodies, all hands, movements framed
in the windows together, reaching up,
all singing "Allah!"